Samuel Proctor: My Moral Odyssey

Samuel Proctor: My Moral Odyssey

Foreword by Bill Moyers

Judson Press® Valley Forge

MY MORAL ODYSSEY

LIBRARY OF CONGRESS
Library of Congress Cataloging-in-Publication Data

Proctor, Samuel D.
    Samuel Proctor: My moral odyssey / by Samuel D. Proctor.
    p. cm.
    ISBN 0-8710-1151-X: $10.95
    1. Proctor, Samuel D. 2. Afro-American Baptists—Biography.
3. Baptists—United States—Clergy—Biography. 4. College
presidents—United States—Biography. I. Title.
BX6455.P76A3 1989
286'.1'092—dc20
[B]   89-38310
                                                                      CIP

The name JUDSON PRESS is registered as a trademark in the U.S. Patent Office.
Printed in the U.S.A.

Dedicated in loving memory
to
Stella Hill Tate
Velma Hughes Proctor
Stuart Maurice Tate
Herbert Quincy Proctor

ACKNOWLEDGMENTS

"I owe a great debt to Dr. Milton Schwebel and Dr. James Wheeler who gave me the opportunity to spend fifteen years in the Graduate School of Education at Rutgers University and to the good people of the Abyssinian Baptist Church of Harlem for allowing me to share my life with them for seventeen years. For forty-four years, 1944-1989, I have been privileged to serve with one foot in the academy and the other in the church. From these two perspectives of life, learning and moral consciousness have been viewed with patient, intensive, tedious, disciplined and humbling observation. This has been done, of course, within the limits of my capacity. These pages are the result of my reflections upon such observations, with the earnest hope that they may encourage others to help in the urgent task of defining the moral life in a time of moral confusion.

While I am totally responsible for what is said here, I am grateful to Bill Moyers for the foreword and to several who read the manuscript and made helpful suggestions: Dr. Calvin Butts, Dr. Jean Dorgan, Reverend Derrick Harkins, Addison King, Dr. Gordon Presley, Dr. Ronald Proctor, Dr. Sandra Proctor, Dr. Olin Robison, Sonca Thompson, Reverend Dino Woodard, and Dr. Jacqueline Young.

My wife Bessie and my sons, Herbert, Timothy, Samuel, and Steven are always called upon first to sample the flow of

7

words and ideas and to save me from the worst mistakes, notwithstanding whatever the results may be. My secretary, Lorraine Smoller, made the task easier with her dedication and encouragement; and throughout the process Esther McCall and Elizabeth Smallwood generously performed added duties at the church. For all of the above I offer my sincere thanks.

SAMUEL D. PROCTOR

CONTENTS

FOREWORD

Sometimes I think Sam Proctor must have lived his entire life on a public platform, speaking. The first time I saw him, he was speaking. The last time I saw him, he was speaking. Even as I write, it is commencement season in the U.S., and reliable sources tell me that Sam Proctor will deliver more graduate speeches than any other person in the country. Actually, Sam does not just speak. He preaches. Oh, my, how he preaches. He is a born preacher. And I am certain that when the Pearly Gates swing open and Sam strides through to claim his richly deserved crown, the first question he will put to Saint Peter will be: "Where's the pulpit?"

And why not? This is not Holmes's frail clergyman "with a one-story intellect and a one-horse vocabulary." Sam Proctor, like those learned men of *Piers Plowman,* lives as he teaches. His life is his best sermon, and when he preaches, it is with "the deep soul-moving sense of religious eloquence" that comes from a life whose doctrine is squared with deeds.

Sam grew up in a family as old-fashioned as flatirons, oil lamps, and graphophones. Even today as he recalls that "warm happy incubator with high moral expectations," he does so with reverence for the hot kitchen on a sultry Sunday, with "warm sweet rolls and the popping of the grease cooking fish and the family around the table." Here was his safe harbor against a world shot through with vice, crime, racism, and

11

cheap tricks. Here he was vastly loved, and here he found "the most fortunate starting point for moral growth and development."

He would need it. There were trials ahead for Sam Proctor. The playboy competed with the preacher for his soul. He would have to spend more time at seminary on his knees, scrubbing the kitchen floors, than he would praying; he was, after all, "colored." He would live his first thirty-four years under the Supreme Court's Plessy vs. Ferguson decision permitting states to deny him access to libraries, rest rooms, theaters, and hospitals. A tiny hole in the ventricular septum of his son's heart almost cost the boy his life because a local ordinance prohibited the Red Cross from collecting "colored blood."

One might expect from all this—and I have mentioned but a few of the impediments he encountered—a soul grown weary with the gauntlet. Or one whose message by now would be one long and loud damnation. Or one of grave and furrowed brow. Why, when Sam Proctor was a college president, he even had Jesse Jackson as student body president—better the plagues of Job!

But nothing shrill or pitying or bitter issues from the pulpit when Sam Proctor preaches. Nor will you find in this book any poisoned wells. You will find grace, courage, wisdom, and humor. At times his voice is one of God's trombones. Other times it chuckles. There was the occasion when he was to speak on racial justice at a university in the deep and segregated South. Times were tense, and who could tell what awaited the preacher? Sure enough, as Sam stood up to speak, a male student emerged screaming from the wing and ran across the stage, completely naked—a "streaker," come to put this black man on edge. Sam Proctor paused. Then he said: "Are there any other volunteers before I go on?" And he held them in the palm of his hand.

I met Sam in the early sixties, when we were deputies to Sargent Shriver at the Peace Corps. Both of us were trained as Baptist ministers, drawn to John F. Kennedy's New Frontier in an effort to relate our faith to the public square. It was said we both possessed somewhat overwrought Baptist consciences, but that was disguise. Sam could turn a meeting around with the right line at the right moment, and I had a penchant for practical jokes. Sam thought sending him—a black man—to direct our program in Nigeria—with 695 white, middle-class teachers—was the biggest practical joke of all. The civil rights movement was nearing its zenith, and Sam was criticized in some quarters for going abroad as the struggle intensified at home. But during the gathering protest this man had roamed the South, speaking several times a week on "The Power of an Idea Whose Time Had Come." And now Shriver was asking him to be ahead of his time—to go to Africa and demonstrate what the movement was about. A black man, an educator and minister, at the head of the largest contingent of white volunteers in Africa. What sermon could match the power of the example?

For the last dozen or so years now Sam has been both pastor of Harlem's famed Abyssinian Baptist Church—founded when Thomas Jefferson was president (and a slaveowner)— and a professor of Rutgers University in New Jersey, teaching "Studies in Afro-American Education." Here he has been exploring, semester after semester, with teachers from throughout the region, one of the stickiest and thorniest problems yet to challenge our country—how to penetrate the ghetto walls and engage the minds of our desperate youths. This is so much the Sam Proctor I know—practicing and preaching, learning and sharing, wrestling demons even as he speaks with the tongue of angels. For the moral odyssey of Samuel Proctor has been to live a whole life in a fractured world, to grow faith in hard places.

The odyssey is not over. Somewhere out there, at this very minute, Sam is on an airplane, heading for another commencement and another congregation. What a treat is in store for the audience in waiting. The man they are about to experience is the boy who once asked his father: "Daddy, how do I know that I am really myself? Am I the only one of me?"

Alas, Sam—alas for all who have not yet heard the message—there is only one of you, and our span of time is short. But consider what you have wrought! Like the meal of loaves and fishes, you have nourished the multitude and lived your life as a miracle.

BILL MOYERS
May 1989

A MORAL ODYSSEY

Beginning in Huntersville

The moral fiber of our society has been unraveling for some time now. There have always been moral failures and lapses in human decency here and there, but what concerns us now is that the standards for moral living have become confused, and we are hearing an uncertain sound that calls us to goodness.

This confusion of values in our society has reached crisis proportions. The troubling statistics on violent crime, drug abuse, and the failure of our families and other institutions are obvious and depressing. Impersonal urban anonymity, rootlessness and high mobility, avid consumerism and materialism, world tensions and militarism, and the idolatrous hedonism that is permeating our culture make it difficult to maintain moral consistency, mental poise, and emotional tranquility.

The issue is further complicated by an atmosphere of uncertain national official commitment, the moral neutrality of schools and colleges, personal moral failure in high places, frequent revelations of dishonesty as government policy, and the threat of a nuclear holocaust as a reality. Many persons are confused and do not know what to believe in as a reliable moral guide.

Notwithstanding, life must go on. And even those who are pledged to Christian discipleship and whose devotion to the

15

mind of Christ is unquestioned find themselves uncertain as moral choices become more complicated and popular pressures are inescapable.

We all need to be equipped with a well-grounded, defensible, and authentic system of values to serve as our moral monitor, a well-equipped conscience with a sensitive, finely tuned signal apparatus.

Fortunately, many have just such a value system as the outcome of their religious training and experience and of their nurture in a religious family and/or church fellowship. For many such a system of values is well in place indeed. For others it has evolved out of slow and tedious stages of moral development that are parallel to similar stages of cognitive and spiritual development. This is where we acknowledge the contributions of three outstanding thinkers: Jean Piaget, Lawrence Kohlberg, and James Gustafson. In their writings they have charted various stages in cognitive, moral, and faith development. Others have had dramatic spiritual experiences that have altered their patterns of living, and from such experiences they derived a value system.

Jean Piaget, the Swiss psychologist, presented an approach to cognitive development that followed certain sequential stages, one building on the other. Lawrence Kohlberg of Harvard has presented a similar development in moral thinking and discernment, and James Gustafson of Chicago has done the same for faith development.

The following essays borrow from these insights of Piaget, Kohlberg, and Gustafson in presenting a life story of developing moral understanding and experience, resulting in a moral frame of reference that may be helpful to others. This moral frame of reference originated in a Christian home and has been supported, nurtured, and validated in Christian service and participation. It is also compatible with the noble surmises that underlie our civic and political experience; our Constitution; our Declaration of Independence; and the ideals of a free, pluralistic, and democratic society. The autobiographical, subjective, and chronological nature of this discussion may be regarded as a kind of odyssey, one further effort to achieve clarification in a complex, moral environment. We must appeal to whatever strategies and methods that are available to contribute to the strengthening of the moral fiber of our society. We have seen that panic responses and "quick-fix" remedies have little effect.

Many persons have never given thought to the question of the source of their own values and simply live from day to day on the basis of conventional, acceptable behavior. However, most of us have our own story to tell about how we accumulated the reservoir of values that give moral ballast, as well as emotional and spiritual fulfillment, to life. No person can boast of perfection, and a continuous practice of confession and repentance, along with the awareness of forgiveness and restoration, must accompany our journey. And we learn from each other. As a boy I felt that something was reaching for my soul as I read the life of Helen Keller, the sightless genius, and the story of Booker T. Washington, with no money, walking from the Blue Ridge Mountains to the Chesapeake Bay to beg his way into college. When I read the lives of Frederick Douglass, Madam Curie, and Harriet Tubman, the mental and emotional tides overflowed within me and the world became a different place.

The chapters that follow describe my moral odyssey beginning in Huntersville, my particular starting point, my unique historical position, within the parameters of one fairly normal life. It is told from within with full apologies. It is a serious effort to capture the flavor of the thought of Piaget, Kohlberg, and Gustafson, and that of countless patient grandmothers, Aunt Marys, and Uncle Richards who have observed the same process but were not scholars and therefore never articulated it or attempted to document its validity. The only proof they had was in the lives of the young over whom they prayed and for whom they gave selfless devotion. If what is said will cause a deeper reflection upon where our values come from, how they are nurtured and celebrated, when and how they should be applied, and how they can be shared with those who are mired in the morass of moral confusion, it will be well worth the effort. In the words of the great apostle

> Finally, . . . whatsoever things are true, whatsoever things are honest, whatsoever things are just, whatsoever things are pure, whatsoever things are lovely, whatsoever things are of good report; if there be any virtue, and if there be any praise, think on these things (Philippians 4:8).

SAMUEL D. PROCTOR
January 1, 1989

1

DISCOVERING
My Own Personhood

THE FAMILY
AS MY MORAL INCUBATOR

One of the first questions that I can remember asking my father was, "Daddy, how do I know that I am really myself? Am I the only one of *me?*" It seemed like such a silly question that I kept it sealed from others; but Daddy would never embarrass me. This question came from those vacant moments that invited introspection, on a dark rainy day when the house was quiet and there was nothing better to do than gaze idly at our thick, leafy "chainey-ball" tree. Loud thunder and sharp lightning convinced me of my human finiteness and brought on questions such as, "Who am I?" I wondered if I could be someone else in another place and time, or if there really was another "me" somewhere else. A feeling of tentativeness followed me while I tried to settle on my real identity and to be certain that the real me was not an Eskimo boy in the Arctic, a Native American in Arizona, a Pilgrim in 1620, or a slave in Tennessee in 1810. I needed some certitude to get me to settle down and go on and live out the days stretched before me in the 1920s in Huntersville, a small, dusty bottom in Norfolk, Virginia.

Such a question is the earliest evidence of the marvelous agility of the human mind, the curiosity that takes nothing for granted, that allows questions to linger until certainty is slowly assured. And our own existence is the first hypothesis to be held up for close scrutiny: "Am I the real me?"

The problem comes, however, when we keep this question unresolved too long, and we find ourselves deferring that moment when we settle down and affirm the fact that we are not someone else, that we are the "original" of who we are, and that no one else was born of the same parents, on the same date, at the same place. Like it or not, I was the real Sam Proctor with all of my private historical data confirmed, with my unique DNA and blood type, and with my own moral incubator in which to interact with parents, brothers, sister, aunts, neighbors, and buddies on the block. There was no escape. I had to affirm this personhood that had been conferred upon me. I was not a statistic, a digit, a shell, a cube, a bundle of tangled instincts and drives; but a thinking, reflecting, remembering, reacting, feeling, analyzing, choosing human being, a unique creation of a loving, eternal, holy God. There are many places to start, as we seek to understand moral growth and development, but in order for us to follow at least this one case study, I must begin at the point where I discovered my own individuality and when I acknowledged, affirmed, and celebrated my own personhood.

It is strange how after so many years the task of piecing together the fragments of Huntersville seems manageable. There is a temptation to romanticize those days, but even a slightly fictionalized narrative that bears the point is worth reporting in the interest of establishing a basis for moral understanding. The earliest recollection of moral experience, honoring the distinction between right and wrong, was that it was simple: it was to obey or not to obey the authority figures at home or in the neighborhood, those who could inflict punishment or deprivation for disobedience. They had all reached a consensus about the good life and how it was to be lived. This consensus was a blend of the Ten Commandments, the teaching of Jesus, and the values of middle-class strivers. My block was populated with at least thirty adults who had absolute control over me, and the earliest experience of moral choice was whether or not to meet their expectations.

These adults were churchgoers, homeowners, and law-abiding, prudent, proud people. Most had migrated into Norfolk from tidewater fishing and oystering counties or from peanut and tobacco farms in Southside Virginia and nearby eastern North Carolina. They were the heirs of earnest political and educational leadership among blacks during the Reconstruction. They wore shined shoes and neckties even on Saturdays. They belonged to social and fraternal groups and were familiar with the Bible, Tennyson, William Cullen Bryant, Longfellow, and Roberts' Rules of Order. The leaders among them had been taught at a United Presbyterian mission college whose faculty stressed music, Latin, the Bible, rhetoric, and personal discipline.

The house at 918 Fremont Street, in which my five brothers, my sister, and I were reared, was built in 1919 under a plan by which Hampton Institute students performed a kind of internship in the building trades, working with black builders in the summer. It was built by my maternal grandfather, a carpenter, Baptist deacon, and choirmaster.

Everyone is born into a physical environment, and everyone inherits a moral incubator as well. Before we are able to make conscious moral choices, we are subject to a moral orientation that is unconsciously recorded on our mental computer; and that recording is made indelible when we associate it with love and caring, loyalty and appreciation. A warm, happy incubator, with high moral expectations and consistent rewards and reinforcements for approved behavior, is the most fortunate starting point for moral growth and development.

In the present day, clearly, with high mobility, the disintegration of family life, and confusion in moral authority, such incubators will be more and more difficult to create and to maintain. As the evidence continues to mount—that such incubators are altogether too rare—the need will become urgent to invent compensatory strategies. We may even have to cre-

21

ate surrogate moral incubators, as our resources, our competence and our commitments may allow. One purpose of this discussion is to alert those concerned to the significance of the difference between outcomes in the lives of those who had adequate incubators and those who did not.

At 918 Fremont Street there was not a lot of money but an awful lot of love. The rearing of children was the major enterprise of the household, and the care and attention seemed inexhaustible. Mamma was perpetually sewing and laundering to keep us looking nice and continually cooking all of the "goodies" that she knew we loved. Where she found the time and strength remains a mystery. Without much money Daddy made toys. He was a gifted craftsman, and he could salvage an abandoned clarinet, build an indestructible wagon, make a sturdy swing, construct a boat, produce a "new" bicycle out of junk parts, and create a doll house with miniature furniture for my sister. Other children were always welcomed in the backyard and at the table with us for any meal. There seemed to be enough always.

Education and mental challenge were part of the steady fare. Every weeknight there were six pairs of elbows at a round dining room table. Poems were memorized, music learned, problems in math worked out by a "committee," compositions drafted, graphs and charts tediously produced, and giggling kept to a minimum. There was a tacit understanding that life was precious, the mind a gift, and childhood the time for development. Not every family sponsored such endeavor. I remember the guilt I felt in school when I observed children who never had their homework, whose parents were too poorly educated to help them, and whose neighbors did not believe in the importance of schooling. These children were slow in attaining the life of the mind.

Work was honored, and it was associated with well-being, not social inferiority. There were house chores for everyone from the very early ages. The boys understood that as their desires and tastes called for more cash, the answer was a better-paying part-time job. From age twelve we had jobs, and

we all worked our way through college and graduate school.
We were taught that to be independent was a matter of pride
and dignity. We understood racism and discrimination and
decided not to roll over for dead until things changed. We
wanted to be prepared to help things to change and to be ready
to participate in the changed world. A hardworking father and
mother gave credence to the value and worth of work.

Sunday was a very special day. We were not sent to Sunday
school. We were carried by my father. We had to study the
lesson and rehearse the music. Daddy played the violin, one
brother played the tuba, and I played the clarinet. We had a
full orchestra in the Sunday school, and we rehearsed each
week. Many other families participated in church life and
gave children the benefit of religious instruction. But it was
obvious also that many other children lived without any contact with institutional religion, and their lives were controlled
by "street" wisdom. The violence and early incarceration for
many of my peers were the consequence of such lack of opportunity. Sadly, the class stratification was apparent to me at an
early age, and those more privileged enjoyed a cluster of education, discipline, and religious participation. Their sin was
often snobbishness.

Personhood is a dynamic concept. One does not make this
discovery and then consider that it is a permanent given. The
discovery that one is more than a package of chemicals is an
important human achievement that requires nurture and sus-
tenance. There is a kind of atavistic drag on human nature
that threatens constantly to deprive us of the freedom and
moral sensitivity that real personhood embraces. Competition
for success and security can make us cunning, avaricious, and
numb to decency. Hedonism and narcissism can stifle appreciation for others and openness to altruistic participation. The
love of thrills and the love of self make machines of us, and
personhood thereby is denied.

Personhood is best nurtured and fostered at an early age in
a family—or a surrogate family environment—where one is
encouraged to cultivate imagination, to set goals and organize

life for his or her achievement, to ask penetrating questions in a nonthreatening atmosphere, to test hunches and insights without fear of failure, and to piece together an understanding of the world that may be subject to revision as new knowledge and experience unfold. A warm and loving "nest" encourages such freedom and creativity and gives one the moral posture for making choices and appreciating moral options.

REINFORCING LINKAGES
BEYOND MY HOME

Beyond the home and family there are usually secondary linkages that become tests for early sampling of the wider world. The postman, I recall, was a daily challenge, and what child has not wanted to sample the outside world by trying the mail carrier among the very first outsiders? Does he or she smile? Is he or she too busy to exchange a few words? Is she or he a parent, too? Mr. Tony Brewington, our mailman, will never know how important his smile was to me.

The basic, primary linkages that we found were in the immediate, nuclear family. It was inescapable also, in a large family, to have other relatives temporarily sharing the home, especially in the Great Depression. Each one of such kin was different, and it was a challenge to learn the levels of tolerance that each had and in what regard. In this daily interchange in the home one found practice in self-assertion, in being a person—a choosing, thinking, reflective being who will make moral choices for seven more decades or better. With these family linkages and among siblings the water was tested.

My grandmother, a former slave who had been sent to college by her family's former owners, was for me a primary linkage. She cared a great deal about the growth and development of children, reflecting her training at the hands of the abolitionist United Presbyterians in the 1870s. She could get furious over the misuse of a pronoun or the incorrect person and number of a verb. And on Sunday if we "faked" illness and tried to avoid church, she would compel us to drink a small bottle of castor oil and remain immobile all day on the Lord's day!

It seems strange to me that I can recall how some of my young peers entered the larger world beyond the home with awkward and underdeveloped social skills, poorly prepared to negotiate, to play a game fairly, to learn a song, or to make a new friend. There had been little affirmation of personhood for them, and those early explorations were clumsy indeed. Some, I recall, never did manage to cope with the real world and make tough moral choices. My parents had brothers and sisters, seven and six respectively, and most had several children. There was abundant opportunity among bloodkin to test my sense of self, to experiment with other selves, to negotiate for turf and mutual survival in a relatively safe circle.

The happiest moments of all were spent with those adults who had patience and time for children. Mr. Otis Petty, the ice man, would let us ride on his wagon and hold the reins and guide the horse; Lawyer Foreman would let me ride with him to his office and use his typewriter, stapler, and rubber stamps; Mr. John Gale would let us go behind the counter in his store and ring the cash register; and Uncle Herbert would let us spin around on his barber chairs, after he had closed, when the white customers were out of the shop and the curtains were drawn.

My heart bleeds for children today who live in neighborhoods where life is so cramped and there is so little trust that children do not have these linkages with adults that are safe and unthreatening and through which they could ease their way without trauma into a stronger sense of self. I have always envied farm children who had a chance to work next to parents every day in fields and barns and share the full range of adult life at work. In my early years it was common for a neighbor to take special interest in a favorite child and make available special trips to shops, to the waterfront, to the farms out of town, and to curious places like the naval base and the huge coal pier at Lambert's Point, where foreign ships were loaded with coal from West Virginia and Kentucky.

Learning how to obey the rules of adult company and maintain approval among them was one of the earliest lessons learned. Getting invited again was the ultimate test. All these experiences called for self-criticism and evaluation; an awareness of oneself as a *person,* not a *thing,* as a *thou,* not an *it.* Earning approval from other adults was one of the first experiences outside of the family. In all these linkages, the primary ones in the family and the secondary ones beyond the blood-kin, we were looking for verification and reinforcement of our understanding of life and how it was to be lived.

Of course, there were disappointments. It hurt to hear rumors of moral failure or to eavesdrop on grown folks' conversations that detailed how a neighbor, a relative, or friend had drifted astray. Yet all of this was instructive. Because of my own personhood I was compelled to make my own judgments on these matters. I felt genuinely sorry for most of them. For others the scandal seemed well deserved and a just reward.

However, the failures were known as such, and despite them the basic moral ideal remained intact. Failures within the larger, extended family were sporadic, confusing, and disheartening, but the standard remained untouched. In the little community there was a domestic brawl here, an arrest there, now and then a child born out of wedlock, a lawsuit, or a job lost for malfeasance; these things got out—a divorce or a sneaking affair among the "worthies." But it was clearly understood that these were violations and that the basic values prevailed. Therefore, even in a negative way these primary and secondary linkages with humanity allowed one to observe the significance of being oneself, directed from within, guided by one's own loyalties and assumptions, objectivizing life and making assessments all the time.

It is clear, up to this point, how essential those early years of moral orientation were in the home and in the church. Today, with so many homes in chaos, so many families fragmented or dissolved, and such high mobility that linkages are weak and temporary, we face the urgent task of compensating somehow for this basic absence of moral introduction in the home and the church. Something has to be done through schools in a nonsectarian mode; but, more fundamentally, home, family, and church have to reestablish the incubator for the human infant, even in a very complicated, litigious, and politicized society.

AN INCUBATOR OF
CONSISTENCY AND COHERENCE

In order for one to make sense of his or her existence, the setting, the environment, must remain in place for a while until names and labels can be assigned and remembered. A young mind takes the world as something dangerous and to be avoided if it keeps turning, jerking, warbling, and landing upside down. I cannot be certain at all as to why we have a teenage suicide problem, a drug epidemic in schools and colleges, and jails running over, but it is clear that when everything stays in flux, values are hard to define, and affirming one's role is even harder to perform.

An infant's mental computer, we are told, stays on and does not lose any data. A record is always being made of the persons, movements, lights, shadows, temperature, and congeniality of the environment. And all of this is responded to overtly or in the unconscious labyrinths of the rapidly growing brain. Moral outlooks are shaping up earlier than we find it comfortable to believe. And at a later date, when tough questions have to be asked—and when there are more symbols and labels available to keep track of things—it must be awful to find the world still shaky, temporary, unreliable, inconsistent, and incoherent. The best atmosphere in which one takes a risk and proclaims his or her separate existence as a person is characterized by consistency, dependability, and coherence. Things must be depended on. What a shock it was to me when I found out simply that my daddy could *forget!* I had learned to depend upon him like the movement of the tides and the daily ascent of the sun toward the meridian, until the day he told me that he simply forgot to get from the repair shop my shoes with thick, new leather heels and huge steel plates attached.

Parents, therefore, have such an important responsibility to the young child to present a world to him or her that he or she can rely upon, with protection from traumatic interruptions; food and warmth provided with dependability; responses to questions that encourage more questions; and behavior that has some recognizable pattern. Unexplained, long absences; unpredictable temper flares; silences that announce boredom and disgust; denial of play and song; the abrupt appearances of strangers, in charge, with no transition to explain their presence; drunkenness; fighting; loud music or conversation—all of these world-shattering, inconsistent vagaries disturb the incubator.

In a large family one faces a world that must be organized into patterns. The home was my mother's domain. She never seemed to question her position. But chores were assigned to all of us. I knew early whom to obey. My older sister and my young aunt were in full charge of the younger boys. Toys, candy, clothes, and tasks were shared from an early age. Bringing in wood, dusting furniture, picking up the backyard, feeding the dog, and answering the phone and the front door were the earliest. And the rewards for good performance were hugs and kisses, compliments before other adults, cookies, candy, figs, pears, and a chance to scrape the sweet potato pie batter from the pan or to lick the dasher from the ice-cream freezer when it was lifted out—on holidays only!

Young adults treated their seniors with deference and respect, and so did we. Profanity was not used in the home, and when we heard it outside, we recognized it and made a quick assessment of those using it. My father played music, rehearsed at home, and started us out with music. He studied the Sunday school quarterly, and we found it consistent to do so ourselves. His friends were self-respecting, and we looked for the same among ours. There was a theme to everything. It was a tacit, implicit "You are somebody." There was another brand of behavior on display in the neighborhood, but it was understood that it was "different." There was more pity than scorn shown toward those who did not live in an atmosphere of consistency.

Daddy had few clothes, and he pressed them himself. His shoes stayed shined, and ours did, too. He used English correctly, and we had to do so also. He read, and we did, too. My mother spoke with compassion and empathy about persons having misfortunes, and she cried a lot in our presence. So tears meant something in our world, and we saw strength, not weakness, in the ability to enter another's sorrow or pain with tears.

Across the street were families similarly oriented, and around the corner there were more. In between, some were quite different, having had weaker influences. But we learned the difference early, and we were held accountable by those women and men who shared the consistent and dependable behavior of our parents. At least twenty of my neighborhood's adults had the unwritten license to chastise and punish us for misbehavior. And when they had to, we got it again when Daddy got home.

Many will recognize this environment and will attest to the discipline that it instilled. However, the point here is that when the child is in search of self, such an environment holds things in place and allows the child to step on board the world with assurance and confidence. It amazes me that beneath the veneer of poverty and racism in that community, men and women who were maids, porters, waiters, longshoremen, freight handlers, and truck drivers—excluded from the mainstream of America and stigmatized by racial discrimination—held their heads high, educated their children, built their institutions, and preferred a life of consistency, discipline, and coherence. Yet alongside them were others who were mired in futility and ignorance, owing to a long period of impoverished tenant farming before coming to the city.

The tragedy is that today we are terribly slow in trying to reach young people whose sense of self was shaped in a motley environment of unpredictable events and behavior, that is

29

reflected in their defiant and reckless approach to life and learning. This loss must be compensated for, even if it means creating entirely new institutions to provide surrogate parenting. We are in a crisis, and the only answer being proposed is more jails. A better answer is to find ways of recovering in the losers an affirmation of their personhood.

The world will not remain orderly, and the strange sights and sounds will not always be so easily recognizable, but the sense of security and the awareness of one's own personhood—not a statistic, an echo, a shadow, or an IT, but a THOU!—that one discovered in those formative years, when the computer was working fast, enable one to bring to the moment of moral choice a steadiness and a poise equal to the challenge.

A WORLD OF ORDER
AND MEANING

A crucial characteristic of the incubator that fosters the affirmation of one's personhood is that one looks around and sees in it order and meaning. Obviously, a young child is unable to grasp the totality of the bad news that may be circulating all around his or her life, but whatever part of the world that he or she can grasp needs to reflect the kind of order and meaning that invites assurance and trust. The most cruel thing that can happen to a young mind is to clutter it with great doubts and to hold before it a meaningless mosaic of strong sights and sounds that have no meaning.

There was a custom in our town of having in the home a wake for the departed member of the family, with a grey crepe hanging at the front door. The casket was brought in the night before the funeral, and relatives and friends spent most of the night in soft, consoling conversation. Death was a terrifying mystery to us, but we were not left to wonder about it on our own. One adult after another assured us that Aunt Nannie was asleep and her soul had gone to be with Jesus. And we were further assured that if we lived a good life we would see her again someday, after we had grown old. When the death occurred tragically or at a pitifully early age, we were assured that though we loved Cousin Bob, God loved him best and God was infinitely wiser than we were. Our world remained intact. We could face the next day with reasonable hope.

Moreover, the sabbath was the Lord's day. Only essential work was done. Those who loved the Lord honored this sacred day. On a sultry, summer Sunday morning in Huntersville all the windows were open; half-screens that would slide to fit most windows kept the flies humming to get in. The dough that had been rising through the night was folded into rolls and put in an oven that made the kitchen too hot for the uninitiated to endure. Fresh Ocean View spots, a sweet-tasting fish available in abundance for the poor, were frying in deep, bubbling grease. And at the appointed moment all eight of us sat down, with hands folded and eyes shut tight, heard Daddy pray without any shame at all that we were grateful for a bright new sabbath, and like Job of old plead for the forgiveness of all of our sins—acknowledged and otherwise. He prayed a regular prayer that we all memorized, and it covered all points. As we ate those delicious rolls, with butter seeping out of the folds, and picked chunks of hot, sweet meat from the fish, we could hear the Wings over Jordan Choir with deep, sonorous voices and close, moving harmony singing their theme song:

> Shine on me, shine on me.
> Let the light from the lighthouse,
> Shine on me.

Indeed, throughout the South from 1921 to 1927, there were lynchings. Blacks were denied the ballot; there was inequality in education, housing, and employment; and police brutality and blatant, official, legal racism were present. But that hot kitchen, Daddy's sabbath prayer, Mamma's sweet rolls, the popping of the grease cooking fish, and the melodious harmony of "Shine on Me" floating into the window sufficiently immunized us from the worst of the news and kept our world in order. God was in ultimate charge.

In addition to all that happened at home, at our church the most successful blacks in town were present teaching Sunday school—the attorney, our physician and dentist, the highest-placed government employees, the teachers, and the principal. And they behaved with the strictest decorum: the music they played well; announcements were made in military precision; the preacher was always well rehearsed, dressed in a long coat, a high collar, and striped, morning trousers. The choir was robed and in place, and my Daddy was on the end singing tenor.

Many of our teachers were public school teachers also. They had finished the black public colleges and church-related colleges, and they understood that teaching Sunday school was a part of their community obligation. They were all local successes, having come from families in the church. Of course, there were many of my friends who were outside of this scene looking in. We passed them on our way to church. Their world was fragmented with alcoholic parents, deep poverty, and few role models that they could touch and feel.

While even with such an incubator, nothing is guaranteed, we do have some idea of what it takes to launch a young life on the open seas of life. The starting point is a positive sense of self. Often it is found in poverty and isolation and in spite of them; often it is missed where there are affluence and abundance. However we manage to provide it, the journey must begin with an awareness of love and caring, positive relations with others, consistency and coherence in the environment, and a world of order and meaning.

Whether the child enters this world on an Iowa wheat farm, a public housing project in Atlanta, a plush estate in Westchester County, a neatly scrubbed row house in Baltimore, or a dusty tenant farm in Oklahoma, with one parent or two, he or she enters with the same equipment, the same neurological apparatus, the same cognitive computer, and the same sense of awe and wonder that every other human infant possesses. Our society must become more aware of the explosive nature of this human package and the care that must be taken to prepare it for a life of intelligent and responsible behavior in a free, democratic, pluralistic society. Our specialists will always be able to inform us on the consequences of our failure. But the problem lies in putting together the appropriate incubator in the first place and reducing the risks and the moral incompetence.

We cannot afford to succeed in our military supremacy, maintain our indulgent lifestyle, enjoy our freedoms, and then continue to drift into such moral chaos that the leaders of our institutions cannot be trusted, our young destroy themselves, our schools cannot function, and we cannot find a bugler to sound a certain sound. All of this must be changed, starting with the nest that encourages the affirmation of personhood.

2
ENTERING
the Life of the Mind

PREPARATION FOR THE
WORLD OF IDEAS

The most wonderful discovery that the growing child makes is the ability to express thoughts and ideas in sentences. And when these sentences are his or her very own, the satisfaction is even deeper. Often I have asked a class in college to pause and make a *sentence* about a certain topic that may be current—say something, anything meaningful about it; and, I get astonished that many persons feel the license only to tell what they have heard or borrowed from someone else. After years and years of schooling, they never entered the world of thought or the life of the mind. They never quite felt free to think with creativity, originality, or independence.

One thing we did at 918 Fremont Street was to play with homemade toys, invent games, and use our imagination freely. We made up stories, and everyone listened and laughed. We made up songs, and we sang and harmonized. My brother Oliver and I would escape to the third floor—the attic—where there was an unused room, and we made a city there out of scraps of lumber—corners cut from two-by-fours wherever building was going on—and the whole family seemed to understand that we were busy playing city and that the people in the city were our fingers. We called it "finger people." In our cities we relived all the experiences of the adult world that we observed. Only now and then did we have cars and trucks from the toy store. We used medicine bottles and blocks of wood whittled and chipped into the likeness of a truck, a wagon, or a car. Often we even painted the wooden "vehicles." I recall hours without measure spent crawling around on the floor pretending to be the ice man, the policeman, the mailman, or the grocery man.

The main thing is that children are allowed to develop vocabulary, to learn to create mental images that are abstract, to try enough new things to require verbs, adverbs, pronouns, and past participles. They need to learn to live beyond the indicative mood—"I came, I will go, I ate, I am still hungry"—and beyond the imperative mood—"Go, come, eat, stay, sit, rise"—and to learn to live in the subjunctive mood—"I may go and I may not! I may eat or not eat!" This is learning a sense of the "perhaps," an awareness of options.

In order for one to cultivate a moral attitude, it *is* necessary to become aware of options, choices, freedom, and "veto power." One must be able to assess consequences, to make some predictions, to foresee some outcomes and then make some decisions. Many learn this fast at home. Others cultivate the "subjunctive" mood in school; still others never do at all.

Throughout all of these years I have been amazed at persons who were robbed of the chance to enter the life of the mind. They live by instincts, glandular urges, neurological necessities, survival techniques, slogans, clichés, customs, rumors, prejudices, and tribalism. They live the unexamined life, and what saves them is that the social customs bind them firmly so that they generally say and do what is expected and conventional.

Our crime rates rise fastest among persons who never were privileged to enter these important uses of the mind. They demand instant gratification; they have trouble setting priorities and choosing among competing claims. Their lives are one heavy cloud of regret. When one talks with a young drug pusher, a violent criminal, or gang member, one gets the feeling that what is said makes no connection with the wider world of experience. Our prisons are filled with persons reading at levels that are years below the national norms. It is quite clear that better parenting and better education are the prime requisites for stemming the tide of crime.

The kind of parenting that we had as children not only encouraged one to recognize what I have called personhood—a sense of self, a sense of worth, a feeling of approval from within—but it also meant an early induction into the life of the mind. Poverty has many dimensions. It can destroy, or it can drive one to inventiveness. Daddy's navy yard pay did not quite do it; so he was a moonlighter at many things. He wrote obituaries for family funerals throughout the community. He repaired plumbing and electrical appliances. He restored plastered walls and installed doors, screens, and doorbells! He repaired violins, recorked clarinets and saxophones, and restrung banjos and guitars. He repaired his own used cars and helped others with their timing gears, rear-ends, and transmissions. Then, he sang tenor in the glee club, played his violin in the Sunday school orchestra, and substituted for everyone who was absent. He never was absent! Anyone privileged to grow up with such a father cannot escape the influence of such a *positive* response to life. His life was a strong statement about courage, purposiveness, commitment, and achievement.

The fallout from that model is fantastic. Mamma baked bread every day. She cooked fresh vegetables and would make a pie out of whatever happened to be in the damaged boxes that we had to get from the railroad warehouse. Dried prunes, peaches, apples, and pears were standards. If a child grows up in a household that is charged with energy and vitality, where no one is allowed to sleep through it all, where the days are programmed, and where there is no line between work and recreation, between contributing and receiving, between your part and the benefit of all, the net outcome is the cultivation of vocabulary, the stimulation of a sense of inquiry, the freedom to reflect, to criticize, to analyze, and to put your own labels on persons and things. One looks up one day and discovers that he or she has been initiated into the life of the mind, the world of thought.

What is the opposite? A house filled with beer bottles and the stench of alcohol; a lazy program for everyone, each movement counted and measured; children taught to wait for someone to buy whatever they want; everyone eating "junk food" every day; all of the music canned and bought and no one daring to create music; no books read; no newspapers or magazines around; no prayers, no one saying "grace" over a meal; conversation limited to grunts and grunts in reply; no plans for the future; no one able to stop a toilet from running water or a faucet from leaking or able to oil the squeaking hinges on an old door. That is the extreme opposite, with everything in between. Not only is personhood sacrificed, but the life of the mind is too often forfeited also.

Concerning the question of how children's lives turn out in the long run, there are really few mysteries. Recently I lost myself in the reading of the biography of Harry Emerson Fosdick, the stellar preacher in America from 1935 to 1965, the one whose pulpit occupied the center of Protestant thought despite his radical and unconventional biblical views. His books and sermons carried one on an intellectual journey into the realm of ancient history, then into modern psychology, again into the maze of scientific discovery, then over the vast terrain of literature, art, and music. His perimeters of thought were invisible, and his warmhearted faith in God and in the uniqueness of Jesus Christ shone brightly through it all. How do people get that way? Few do! But those who do are the products of a most fortunate set of interventions. Fosdick's father and his grandfather loved learning. They were both school principals and superintendents in Buffalo.

Occasionally, nature, genetics, and environment all meet their match when a person of limited means and stimulation, through sheer grit and guts, rises above it all and makes a game out of high achievement. Thomas A. Edison and Mary McCloud Bethune are prime examples.

Edison spent only three months in the public schools of Port Huron, Michigan, and in 1927 at age eighty he was admitted to the National Academy of Sciences. In his lifetime he secured 1,033 patents for his inventions. In terms of technology, our lives have been affected by the mind of Edison more than anyone else. Who would have thought that when he was selling papers at twelve years of age with a third-grade education? Beneath that image of abject failure was a person of enormous promise.

Mary McCloud Bethune was born in rural South Carolina, one of fifteen children. Both parents had been slaves. In 1904 she founded Bethune-Cookman College in Daytona Beach, Florida. By what genius could she crawl from beneath such a weight of deprivation and become advisor to five successive presidents of the United States? She often spoke of how a book was snatched from her as a child with the admonition that books were not for people "like her."

However, there was an intervention, a certain Emma Wilson, her grade school teacher, who discovered a white Quaker teacher in Denver named Mary Crissmon, who was willing to finance Mary's education at Scotia Seminary in Concord, North Carolina. That did it. There she entered the life of the mind.

THE QUESTIONS
THAT WILL NOT WAIT

All of us, of whatever class or race, must find answers to the same basic questions in life, and every one of us needs the same basic, minimal intellectual capability to deal with them:

1. At the center of this universe, is there a sponsorship friendly to the human condition, or is the world against our best interest? Can I assume that failure for me is not a foregone conclusion? Yes or no? No one escapes this question.

2. Am I well enough prepared to go it on my own, or must I plan to lean on someone else? This demands an answer.

3. Will I play the game of life fairly and squarely, or will I make my own rules as I go along? Will others be able to predict my behavior and count on it? This question *gets answered,* either overtly or tacitly.

4. Do I have goals set for my life that are high enough, demanding enough, all-encompassing enough, fulfilling enough to make this journey worth my while? Tough question, but it will not wait.

5. Shall I contribute to a world of peace, mutual coopera-tion, love, understanding, and a sense of community? Shall I be a part of the answer or another problem?

6. Am I willing to aim for the best and risk failure, or should I take no risks at all and let failure overtake me? It will be answered sooner or later.

These questions remain with us all through life, and our moral maturity is determined by how we deal with them. An uncultivated mind would never grasp the depth or the serious-ness of these questions and stagger through life living out a weak response to all of them. But one who had the good fortune to grow up in a stimulating environment wrestles with such questions for a lifetime; and although one may never be satisfied that they are answered completely, the tentative an-swers are sufficient from day to day.

In Huntersville it was clear that some children were simply living out the kind of trajectory that was established for them at home. The die was cast there. In school they only partially understood what was taught. We could see the teacher giving up on them. Their parents came to school only when sent for by the principal, mostly after a fight. They never volunteered for anything, knew no songs or poems, and laughed defen-sively and without conviction at the others who did know music and poetry.

Not only were they not college bound, but they were des-tined to follow low-paying, temporary, menial jobs and pay rent for cheap dwellings in bad neighborhoods for a lifetime.

In a free society we are *free to fail.* Moreover, we reproduce our kind, and after two or three generations we almost have an underclass.

Well, what will intervene? What breaks this lockstep and causes schooling and learning to be such a joy that poverty will find no one to accept it? Everyone will be prepared for self-reliant, independent living, with a high vision for his or her own life and for the country as a whole. The revolution that we need is one that permits the weakest and most marginal child to find schooling to be the grand intervention in her or his life and a means of induction into the world of thought.

THE PROCESS
OF INTERVENTION

If our schools are going to succeed at this intervention and save us from a growing underclass, the most serious challenge will be for teachers to be freed from the chronic moral hypnosis that has cast such a spell on the total society. We seem to be helplessly hooked on the ethics of Charles Darwin, i.e., the survival of the fittest. In social terms this often means simply the survival of the most privileged and the best-endowed persons.

Darwin's *Origin of Species,* published in 1848, stood the intellectual world on its head. He proposed that human life had evolved from a process of slow biological evolution; following that proclamation, the whole chapter 1 of Genesis shook and trembled. He proposed further that all of human life and all of society took shape and form as the strongest survivors—the strongest persons and the strongest nations, those best able to respond to nature's challenges—gained dominance and ascendency. One can see how this kind of thinking could easily translate into justifying any person, any race, or any nation simply abusing, oppressing, and exploiting another. What could not pass at first in the name of decency and compassion could pass later in the name of the survival of the fittest. Thus, racism, sexism, colonialism, imperialism, and worldwide exploitation of weaker people became quite acceptable.

Jesus and the eighth century B.C. prophets Micah, Amos, and Isaiah all recognized the wickedness of oppression and spoke scornfully of the domination of the rich and the powerful over the poor and the powerless. But somehow Darwin's hold on us lasts, and we seem to prefer to behave as though all of us were in a ruthless, competitive struggle to dominate.

In the schools that I attended in Huntersville, what I recall was how even there the teachers and principals, with the sweetest of intentions, followed Darwin unwittingly and celebrated those children whose successful parents they already knew, children who came from the better homes where there were books, music, and orderliness. These children caused their teachers to look good when they recited, sang solos, or presided in assemblies. I was among them. And I always felt a little guilty that some of my buddies from ill-kept and poverty-ridden homes were so overlooked. It also caused trouble because the school bullies resented us, and we were always challenged to prove that we could fight, too!

The intervention that is called for now could take place dramatically if teachers could be educated to believe that beneath those bad statistics are real persons of promise. God only knows how much mind power has been wasted because teachers were misled by uncombed hair, untied shoes, running noses, and clothes worn too long between launderings. Jesus, with his simple and unmixed compassion toward those who were most marginal, still leads the human race in this regard, and the gap is widening.

An entire social awakening lies dormant at our schools' doorsteps, waiting for the schools of education that train teachers to prepare them to see the world through the eyes of children who have been suffering from racial isolation, endemic poverty, and inward self-rejection. The quality of professionalism needed is marked by "vicariousness," the empathetic participation in the experiences and the world view of another, to be able to understand another's life's situation. The height of professionalism for a dentist, a basketball player, an artist, an architect, a nurse, or a rock singer also is to know the world of one's counterpart, one's client, or one's opponent. It is even more essential for the teacher, the counselor, or the minister of religion to know the world of one's students, counselees, or parishioners.

MAKING LEARNING FUN

Beyond being able to see worth and promise beneath the crust of poverty and otherness is the excitement of seeing others learn and enter the life of the mind. This was the bane of the stiff, formal, Victorian schooling that we endured. It had been imposed upon our teachers, and they passed it on to us. Keeping us quiet was more important to them than exciting us with ideas. It seemed like a great conspiracy to keep us docile and unquestioning.

I recall a lesson in which we were drawing a map of the world and painting all the French colonies blue, the Spanish green, the Belgian purple, the German brown, the Dutch yellow, and leaving the British the color of the paper to save paint! And I remember wondering what the French were doing way down in Equatorial Africa, a long way from Paris; why the Belgians were in hot Stanleyville, the Portuguese in torrid Angola, the Dutch way out in the East Indies and Curaçao, and the Spanish all the way over in Honduras. Such a question would have ruined the whole geography lesson, but my curiosity was there.

The educational fraternity is preoccupied with testing, with quantitative standardization, but persons who enter the schooling process from intellectual numbness need time for questioning, exploration, and experimentation. Learning is very exciting stuff, and it can be emotional, noisy, and not so easily or quickly measured. For the uninitiated it needs to be nurtured with care.

I recall that every language that I have studied has at least two verbs that are translated "to know." In Latin *cognosco* means "I know" and so does *scio;* in German both *kennen* and *wissen* mean "to know." In French both *connaitre* and *savoir* mean "to know," and in Greek *epistamai* and *gynosko* both mean "I know." In each instance one "to know" means to be acquainted with; to know a label, a name, a place, a date, a number. It means simply to recognize something again and again. In the other instance, "to know" means to understand, to comprehend, to know the taxonomy of something and its relationship to other things. It was one thing, for example, to know where the German, Dutch, British, and Spanish colonies were on the map and their names. It was another thing to understand colonialism, the dominance of Europe over all dark-skinned people who lived near deserts, rain forests, parched and crusted earth, amid overpopulation and pantheistic religions that defied empirical approaches to nature; and who had been overrun by nations that had gunpowder. One "knowing" was like *connaitre*, acquaintance, and the other was like *savoir*, comprehension; one like *cognosco*, identifying, and the other like *scio*, understanding.

We still wonder after nearly two thousand years how persons like John Mark, young Timothy of Lystra, Peter, James, John, and Luke could have had such modest education and lived in such a narrow corner of the world—not in Athens, Alexandria, or Rome—and yet become the vessels of such salient truths about things eternal that they could cause the Pax Romana to become the Holy Roman Empire and cause the name of Jesus of Galilee to supplant the names of all the emperors and to be sung in a thousand tongues.

Persons who have been isolated from the mainstream in the society may not have a fund of ready knowledge to pass standardized tests. They may not have much *cognosco*, but they may have intelligence and can be led into *scio* with excitement and appreciation. Barnabas, Mark, Titus, Timothy, Peter, James, and John could not have passed a test on Plato, Euripides, Sophocles, or the Hyksos dynasties of Egypt. But they had

43

enough *savoir* to confront Hellenic culture, Roman imperialism, and the kaleidoscope of mystery religions to plant the church of Christ in Europe and Asia Minor.

SERVING THOSE WHO
NEED US MOST

It is also curious to observe that all persons, at a very fundamental stage, need to learn the same things. We live under one sky, on one *terra firma,* and the facts are the same in China, Africa, or Borneo. Tides, genes, chemicals, kidneys, hurricanes, algebra, cancers, music, mathematics, and pharmacy are the same everywhere. There is a body of knowledge out there basic to everyone's success in the modern world.

In Nigeria I had 695 Peace Corps teachers to supervise with an extraordinarily able staff. It took no time at all for them to put learning and teaching out front, to generate emancipation and opportunity through knowledge, and to treat such differences as they found in diets, dance steps, and the handling of the dead as cultural differences that had nothing to do with the basic facts that *all* students had to learn the world over. The important fact was that those people who continued to languish in ignorance and illiteracy would remain poor and politically vulnerable, while those who entered the life of the mind would begin that long trek toward self-determination and enlightenment.

Our Huntersville schools did one other significant thing for us: they helped us greatly in developing appreciation for our heritage as black people—only we were "colored" then! We learned who Carter G. Woodson, George Washington Carver, Harriet Tubman, Phyllis Wheatley, Paul Laurence Dunbar, and James Weldon and Rosamond Johnson were. Some of our schools bore the names of black pioneers like J. C. Price and Lott Carey. We learned spirituals and black poetry. All of this pointed us toward self-approval and a stronger posture for facing this society and working for a better day for ourselves and all the oppressed people of the world.

In the 1960s education in America's colleges was challenged to respond to the rejection of Western norms by black students and to include black studies in the curricula to the point of allowing blacks to prepare for a kind of nationalism independent of and apart from their American citizenship. Much of this is now less strident, but it remains.

It is palpably a sad commentary on education in America that such a grudging effort was made to hasten our elevation from the pits of slavery to the plateau of human fulfillment and that college students, often a minority of 3 to 5 percent, would feel compelled to risk going to jail and being expelled in order to alter the curriculum. Such a sluggish and torpid effort was made that the rumor persisted that blacks were genetically inferior; and the chorus of ugly comments about our poverty, our crime, and our social lag perpetuated an insidious black stereotype. All of this is traceable to the paltry effort made to induct us into the life of the mind. We were the victims, and we were then blamed for our own plight. It is the sad fact that every black child born in America today must count as part of his or her legacy the racism that still pervades the land.

Little wonder, then, that many young blacks felt that education meant initiation into a morally decadent culture. Their alienation caused them to view education that was offered as destructive to their sense of self. So they resisted Western definitions of truth, justice, peace, democracy, and freedom and sought another orientation. There is more in this, really, that reflects poorly upon the society and its failure than anything else. Obviously, after all, if these students plan to work and live in the United States, they must know, among all other important and desirable things, what is required of all persons for full participation in this society.

For whatever reason, our Huntersville schools saved us from a sense of futility and prepared us to hold our heads high in the midst of the daily insults. Our education was so grounded in religious faith and practice that the flavor of the gospel was laced through all our schooling. Before the Supreme Court ruling against it, we began each day with prayer and Bible reading or recitations. And we sang hymns in school. All of us were Christian, presumably, and no one seemed offended. There was a sustained spirit of hope, believing that God was in history working things out—a simple, unquestioned, steadfast trust. And if we did our part, God would do the rest. And one day, without doubt, a change would come. This allowed us to live day by day confirmed in our endeavors. I cannot recall any feelings like hatred, resentment, or hostility against any persons or groups, but I did feel deep determination to live and work for change. We lived in a kind of divine parenthesis, with a kind of "not yet" understanding. It was an interim, a piece of "spiritual history," *heilsgeschichte,* * an interlude, an awareness that the whole world was in God's hands, and the end was pending. God had brought Moses and the Israelites through the Red Sea. God had caused the ferocious lions in the den with Daniel to go to sleep; God had insulated the Hebrew boys from the flaming tongues of fire in the furnace. So, if we were faithful and diligent in our duties, the same God would soon stop lynching, bring a halt to segregation, enlarge the franchise, put blacks in Congress and on the Supreme Court, and change this whole wicked world.

When I recall the difference between the way we were taught to think about persons and their moral obligations to each other and to society at large and the way other young people were initiated into moral thinking, it is clear to me that a major intervention must occur. When I conceive of the hundreds of thousands of young people in our prisons for drug-related crimes, murders, rapes, kidnapping, child abuse, and burglary and battery of eighty-year-old women for their welfare checks, and recognize that the incubator that spawned them is still in operation—our cities' slums and the crime schools that those slums have become—it is clear to me again that an intervention is urgent.

*An interpretation of history emphasizing God's saving acts and viewing Jesus Christ as central in redemption.

Persons who live at some distance from this environment may be led to believe that such interventions as Head Start, Job Corps, and college loans are big-ticket items and should be sufficient. These are persons who have no perception at all of the difference between the historical situations of blacks and of European immigrants coming here who were white and joined up with other whites from Budapest, Liverpool, Dublin, Palermo, Leipsig, Amsterdam, and Kiev. Surely, with no money it was not easy, but it is light years from 4 million blacks, emerging from 247 years of slavery; without last names, money or education; laughed at; joked about; treated like chickens, rabbits, and hounds; and branded with the stereotype of a jolly, lazy subspecies. No one knows how long the recovery time is, given the casual and begrudging commitment of the body politic and the society of the white majority. Moreover, when the behavior that such oppression and neglect generate is on display, it offends everyone's sensitivities. It arouses emotional repulsions, and the politicians get elected by promising to support capital punishment and other stiffer penalties. And the kinds of politicians who get elected like that do no more than compound the problem with their total lack of understanding. An intervention is needed.

In America we have already seen the fantastic consequences of intelligent interventions. We defeated both the Germans and the Japanese in World War II, when I was in college. Those countries were paralyzed economically and morally, devastated physically and culturally. Had we waited for the long and tedious process of social and political evolution to bring them back on their feet, they would still be getting CARE packages. But we intervened. We poured in our tax dollars to prop them up again and to nurture them back to strength. Now we are a debtor nation to both of our World War II enemies. Some have laughingly suggested that blacks should have made war against the U.S. and lost, too!

When the land grant colleges and universities were founded with federal monies and with state support, it meant that young people from moderate- and low-income families by the millions could get university education. That was a publicly financed intervention. It worked. Without it we would have a handful of elitists from families able to send them to expensive, private schools. When Israel was born in 1947, that fledgling nation had not a prayer of survival without massive aid. We financed Israel to the full extent of her need, built a wall of fire around her, and dared any of her hostile neighbors to touch her. Intervention? Indeed, and gratefully so. It is the best example of a moral response to an apparently impossible situation.

Now, here we are in America with no plans but bigger jails for the thousands of youngsters who were denied a chance to enter the life of the mind, to assert and affirm their personhood, to learn to use their freedom, to assess their options, to predict their future, and to live lives of higher moral tone.

We need the most comprehensive planning by state education departments, the U.S. Office of Education, the Department of Health and Human Services, the White House staff, the Department of Defense, and assorted sages from the universities and concerned citizens to show how we can stop spending $25,000 to $35,000 a year on the nation's failures, in the prison systems, and spend half that amount to produce citizens, responsible family members, contributors, and *taxpayers!*

We should convert twenty-five of our deactivated military bases into national youth academies for 125,000 of our most troubled and *unparented* youth, ages twelve to eighteen. We must recruit and *retrain* 12,500 of the brightest and most concerned teachers of the nation to spend two to four years as teachers and counselors. After all, we had 16,000 in the Peace Corps in 1964 teaching 6,000 miles away from supermarkets and discos! We must add to their teaching skills the personnel direction of compatible military retirees, the best of the professional athletes like "Dr. J" Erving, Walt "Clyde" Frazier, Althea Gibson, Fran Tarkenton, and "Sugar" Ray Leonard, and others who are specially trained for such service.

These national youth academies would function with closer supervision, tighter fiscal control, better discipline, and more moral education than anything we have seen. All the necessary legal preparation for getting the right young people in—all 125,000—would be accomplished, and other families would pay the going rate to have their children included!

A three-pronged approach to their needs would be in place. First would be a clean, tough curriculum leading to real skills in writing, using computers, and conquering math through calculables for the real world. Everyone would learn to swim in the first month, swimming being the most elementary exercise in overcoming one's environment!

Second, in addition to the curriculum, there would be human development programs and music, music, music, music! There would be intramural sports, drama, gymnastics, mountain climbing, photography, debating—all the things that contribute to the discovery of inner strength and creativity. Days would be full and supervised. Neither could the drug merchant find an opening to sell nor the students the time or energy to sniff, snort, or shoot up. When they got off the clock, they would fall into the arms of Morpheus!

Third, every needed service would be done by the students for pocket money and savings toward graduation—be the service painting, nursing, plumbing, accounting, security patrols, tuning truck motors, growing collard greens, candling eggs, slaughtering cows, cultivating flower gardens, or repairing sidewalks. The students would rotate on jobs and learn everything that an Iowa farm boy knows about tools, work, weather, and responsibility.

Upon graduation, they would go to a community college, to Harvard or Duke or Texas A & M, into the Air Force or the Coast Guard, or enter the world of business and industry, and make room for the next wave.

The net result would be skill development but, more so, the recovery of the moral life of our nation. We do not need to wring our hands in horror at the eleven o'clock news. We need to be intelligent and resourceful in starting anew in inducting into the life of the mind those youngsters who were born without their permission and allowed to grow like weeds, *unparented!*

Even so, some Darwinians would prefer to gas them all. Others of us have heard some haunting words from One who saw beneath the shallow data about people. "Inasmuch as ye have done it unto one of the least of these my brethren, ye have done it unto me" (Matthew 25:40, KJV).

In the summer of 1978 I was recovering from myocardial infarction, and I buried myself in John Rawls's *A Theory of Justice.* He wrote to correct the idea that social justice was doing the greatest good for the greatest numbers. Rawls had a suspicion that the greatest number would end up defining that greatest good to their own advantage. No. He argued for justice as *fairness,* everyone beginning at the same scratch line, playing by the same rules, with no unfair impediments placed in anyone's path, and then let the outcomes fall where they may.

Well, the best that we can do is to *imagine* an "original position" at birth. Obviously, we all do not have the same beginnings, but no one comes here *deserving* or having *earned* or *merited* anything either! We all come here naked, unschooled, helpless, and threatened with extinction. But some land in a position with countless, *unearned blessings,* educated parents, a home with the aroma of the Gospels, high moral tone in the family, and money waiting to sponsor summer camp, trips to Europe, and saxophone and skiing lessons. Others land in alcoholism, an ill-kept tenement, a domestic brawl and semiliteracy, far beneath the imaginary "original position."

At 918 Fremont Street there were limited means for all six pairs of those elbows at the dining room table, but we were far above the original position by inheriting the love of caring parents, faith in the living God, a strong affirmation of our personhood, and an early induction into the life of the mind.

3

USING
My Margin of Freedom

THE BEGINNING OF
SERIOUS MORAL CHOICE

One of the most frightening aspects of growing up is that slow but sure discovery that we do have the freedom to make some serious choices in life on our own, and these choices do not go away. Throughout our early childhood we operate with some simple behavior patterns in mind and within those fixed parameters laid down by parents and parental surrogates. But at about age sixteen our moral monitoring begins to shift from adult control over us to our own control from within. It does not occur in one day or one week. It is like a ship leaving a calm, safe harbor, in full view of the open ocean, but slowly moving through strong sea walls, between rigid jetties, and along sturdy wharves that protect it from the relentless approach of the untiring, pounding, rolling waves. The moment does come in life when all that we have to rely upon are our own rudders, our own propellers, and our own power source. And when these are in disorder or bad repair, we are indeed like a ship lost at sea.

Urban children missed the advantages that rural children had, entering adulthood while working beside their parents, caring for cows, chickens, horses, sheep, goats, and equipment; learning how to meet nature's demands; repairing tools and trucks; predicting rain, snow, frost, and temperatures; assessing the risks of what to plant, where, how much, and when; understanding the market, governmental farm regulations, borrowing and buying at interest rates that vary; wheeling and dealing, bartering and trading with neighbors. There is a quiet wisdom and a ripening of the spirit that is afforded one who lives in the constant presence of nature's most persistent challenges. Then look at what we have lost in trying to induct the young into the real world when they discover milk not in a pail but in a sealed carton; beef in a "Big Mac" and not on the hoof; and wheat not in a field but in a box of pancake mix! There is the irrecoverable loss of the appreciation that we ought to have for nature's processes and provisions.

Leaving 918 Fremont Street for my own open sea, I found myself shining shoes for a nickel a pair, and a nickel tip, at a sleazy barber shop, where poor white customers were served by my aging great uncle, my mother's mother's sister's husband, who was a joke-telling, gentle, carefree alcoholic. He had been widowed for twenty years and did not want or need much money. He drank constantly but bore the appearance of respectability, even while many "sheets in the wind." We were taught to tolerate his condition discreetly. I worked at his barber shop because he liked all children, and especially did he show favoritism toward me. I laughed at all of his stale jokes.

On my first day I discovered that the owner of the shop operated an ostensible corner confectionery also; it was an adjacent room, with an entrance on the street that ran beside the shop. He called me abruptly after my first few hours and told me to go across the street and bring the "baby carriage" back. His wife had it ready. The carriage rattled with the shaking of twenty or thirty pint bottles of prohibited corn whiskey. The barber shop, I learned, was a mere front, and my easygoing, alcoholic great uncle and I were mere decoys. The main business was a bootlegging operation.

My next job was in a more sophisticated shop downtown, well equipped with two skilled and savvy barbers and more shoes to be shined. I was a high school senior by then, but only fifteen, active in band and student government, and president of the senior class. It was a segregated school, and we went about our work with a strong sense of the future. But my barber shop job was a gross incongruity. The customers were only a "cut" above those I had had at the other shop. Yet, despite their slightly higher status, in that barber shop I learned a complete thesaurus of profanity and heard an unbroken refrain of sex stories as the customers competed in describing their extramarital exploits. More than that, at 6:30 P.M. when the shop closed, a special set of clientele—the local Chinese cook, the nearby black auto mechanic, a Philippine naval chief in uniform, the "Wasp" store clerks, a black hotel "maid," and others—comprised an "ecumenical" poker game with "green" money piled high on a table in the back room under a darkly shaded, low-hanging lamp. They paid me two dollars to watch for three or four hours. I lasted only a few weeks before fear of my father finding it out and of a police raid compelled me to quit.

The next job before college, in the summer of 1937, was as a busboy-bellhop at a small Ocean View hotel. That hotel turned out to be a place where beach prostitutes brought naval officers and other more affluent clients. As soon as I left the protected environment of 918 Fremont Street, I found myself confronted with a view of the urban world, emerging out of the Great Depression. It was filled with vice, crime, racism, and cheap tricks. And I had some choosing to do, fast.

Apart from the "education" that I gained in those "sleazy" jobs, I was growing up physically; other responses were called for, and other choices were to be made. The normal, natural drives and urges were present, and either they had to be sublimated by time and energy devoted to enjoyable and challenging activities, or they were left to flood the mind and set the pace for one's life. This is the most troubling time in growing up because peer pressures are so seductive, and one who is unprepared will engage in all sorts of rationalizations and mental torture in trying to manage this crisis. Sex talk, sex jokes, sexual suggestions were as common as breathing, and even subtle invitations to experiment with homosexuality were made by peers and adults.

Parents, pastors, counselors, coaches, teachers, older siblings, and friends need to remain alert to this challenge of the teens and to take it seriously. Fortunately, many of us were so absorbed in orchestras, sandlot football, high school politics, and sufficiently under parental supervision that we escaped teenage parenting and dropping out of school. Many of my peers, however, were not so fortunate.

Today, with contraceptives so available, money so abundant, cars and privacy so easily accessible, and abortions legalized, young people today need even more guidance and support. My generation had no such opportunities for permissive sexual practice, on a steady basis, and the fear of becoming a "child" parent was a powerful inhibitor. Notwithstanding, a life that is controlled by a preoccupation with sexual practice as recreation and a life that is so indulgent as to use another's body as a mere convenience is a living denial of the principle of recognizing full personhood in others. God made persons to become very special beings, created for interpersonal relations quite different from the way mice, rabbits, and frogs mate and reproduce.

Therefore, with parental authority receding and with the adult world of choice pressing hard upon the late adolescent, the tremendous importance of those sixteen years of incubation becomes glaring. Likewise, the quality of that incubation in the home, the church, the community, and the school has an awful lot to do with the direction that a life will take at age sixteen.

Not long ago, I visited two New Jersey prisons to give an address at their graduation programs. In my conversations with the inmates it was clear that it was about at age sixteen that they found that their awareness of their freedom was unmatched by sufficient moral grooming, education, and rehearsal and that the unstructured adult world was mined with moral challenges that they failed to handle successfully. One said to me, "Man, if I had met anybody who talked to me when I was sixteen like you did today, I wouldn't be here in this place for the rest of my life."

Yet despite the pressures and the early negative conditioning for it, one still has the freedom to reject the seduction to destructive behavior and to veto the negative aspects of his or her upbringing. The fact is that countless young people do indeed fail to meet successfully the challenge of the world, like Paul's young follower named Demas, who "loved this present world" (2 Timothy 4:10); yet anyone who spends a career working with the young will know also that many do find and use their freedom and unfetter themselves, correct their mistakes, and live beautiful, reconstructed lives.

WHEN THE MARGIN OF
FREEDOM APPEARS

Moral growth involves the accumulation of moral habits and values from family and other institutions; but it makes its critical leap when it includes the discovery of freedom that allows us to choose to follow the best preparation that one was given, to reject those seductions that would contradict that preparation, and, when failing, to reach out for a new beginning.

Somehow, writing about this seems such a feeble representation of the reality. One would have to see a young mother, at age fourteen, trying to manage an infant while working as a migrant laborer and then see that same young mother, with her child, ten years later, receiving a master's degree in speech pathology and on her way with a full grant for doctoral studies. She found the freedom to veto her past. In order to know the truth about this freedom, one would have to see a college president with gaudy tattoos on each arm, reminiscent of the days when, as a high school dropout, he enlisted in the army and tried to hide from the real world. Knowing these persons and countless others gives one an authentic understanding of the earnestness of this margin of freedom that we have.

When we use this freedom properly, what can we expect to happen? How does it operate? Well, for one thing, we never fully escape the influences of that early "nest"; and if it was successful, we have retained our sense of worth, our basic personhood. Despite those sleazy jobs and the vulgar outlook on life that I witnessed, I knew that I did not want to be poor, ignorant, marginal, or living a life of crime and delinquency. I had been given a sense of worth that defied that total image.

There were three of us of college age at the same time, and my father's income was modest. My sister was given all he had, and to go to college my brother and I were given *permission!* My brother won a music grant to Alabama State College, and times were so tough that he could not get home for four years. I won a music grant to a college closer to home, and with a National Youth Administration job for room and board I made it. Only I wanted to be a lawyer, and I planned to squeeze in enough prelaw electives to get admitted to law school later. That sleazy world of bootleggers, gamblers, and prostitutes that my little navy town had exposed to me dropped out of sight. I was lost among black Ph.D.s from Chicago, Yale, Michigan, Cornell, and Columbia; my clarinet playing continued in the Trojan band of Virginia State College, as did my saxophone chair in our jazz band with Billy Taylor, the famous jazz pianist and commentator, as our accompanist. It was another world altogether.

My sense of worth—not arrogant egotism but full appreciation for human potential as God given—had enabled me to put my freedom to use, to claim my possibilities, to put time and energy at the service of my own objectives, and to put more and more space between the world I chose and the bootleggers, gamblers, and prostitutes that I had fled.

Next, our early moral rearing and the assurance of our own personhood enable us to recognize personhood in others, to respect their worth and dignity and to honor the human potential in them. Incidentally, this is the basis of fairness, democracy, family stability, interracial justice, and world peace! It is seeing in others the worth and dignity that we have affirmed in our own lives. When we fail in this, we have disorder in our world, our nation, and our families.

Freedom allows us to do something about the failure. Many have discovered this worth in others, and many have even pursued this ideal to their death. During the days of the civil rights protests in the 1960s, white persons went to protest sites in the Deep South for the sake of the worth that they saw in others, and they were killed in the most brutal manner. This is what they chose to do with their freedom.

This freedom may be recognized at a much earlier stage, and it may clearly express itself as we recognize worth in others at an early age. Somehow, I recall having such sensitivity to violence that I could never engage in a good fight. Once a schoolmate pushed me in the mud and ruined my starched white trousers. I caught him and banged his head on the school wall until his eyes were out of focus. I went to my desk and cried. My buddies called me a hero, because he was a "bully." I rejected that and all such violence. It defied my notions of personal worth.

In a racial skirmish among schoolchildren I recall some large black fellows stopping a much smaller white boy who was riding a pony. They snatched him from his pony, slapped him to the ground, and whipped his pony. As the pony ran and the boy got up crying, I was so relieved that other students caught his pony and helped him to get on it; and then a fight broke out over that among our group!

Our freedom, used at its best, enables us to respond to the worth that we see in others. The range of choices that awareness of our freedom opens before us is astounding when that freedom is amplified. Our freedom is only partially realized when it is used to promote our own worth; it is flawed and fragmented unless it is put to use also in promoting the worth that we recognize in others.

FREEDOM AND COMMITMENT

In my sophomore year at college I was initiated with high anticipation into a fraternity. But the initiation violated all the regulations of both the college and the fraternity. The "hazing" was brutal and useless; the physical abuse was dangerous and near homicidal. I endured it to save my pride; and I was proud

57

to become a member of that fraternity, even though the few violators of the rules almost turned me back.

This event caused me to undergo the most serious introspection and the most penetrating examination of my basic outlook on life. I will never forget what it was like to have a lifetime friend of my family and mine compel me to stand still and allow him to strike me dozens of times at his full strength with a four-foot oak board. The confusion, the resentment, the disbelief were immeasurable. The revelation of the perversion of human values was shocking.

I lived with this tense resentment until the next initiation. I announced to the group that if they conducted another initiation like mine, I would report *all* fraternities to the president. I knew the penalty. I knew I would be ostracized and threatened. But they did repeat the practice, and I did report them. And I was ostracized by almost everyone and threatened bodily.

It was new to me that I had such courage and that my freedom to move so independently was real. I had never felt so right, so convinced, so certain in my whole young life. I was still only seventeen years old, and those threatening me were much larger than I and about twenty-one years old.

Perhaps most of us can recall that one major event, decision, or crisis that compelled us to use our freedom, to stand alone, to test our moral muscle and to prevail. In one way or another, these Damascus Roads, these burning bushes, these visions of a temple filled with smoke do come, and we drive a stake in the midst of time and mark the moment well. We find the strength to make a clean decision without measuring the consequences. We act as though the most important result is not what flows from the action but the action itself and its intrinsic correctness. We use our freedom.

FREEDOM AND
LONG-RANGE GOALS

Finally, our use of freedom allows us to choose our long-range goals for our lives, to eliminate those subordinate bids for our ultimate loyalty, and to settle on our priority. After my first two years of college, I was in great confusion. My experience with the initiation forced me to revaluate the life chances and options stretched out before me.

Because of World War II, the government was drafting eighteen-year-olds; I chose to enter the Naval Apprentice School rather than risk the draft. President Roosevelt had suddenly issued an antidiscrimination order, and I qualified to be appointed as a shipfitter's apprentice. The money was good, and the security for life assured; but I still had my freedom, and I kept my options open.

Every now and then the vision of becoming a highly paid, well-dressed, local playboy with a diamond ring, a fine home, a handsome car, and a long-delayed marriage with ten years of fun and travel, showing up at homecoming in the latest style with the prettiest available lady on my arm and attending every party with a new face appealed to me. I wanted to try out the high life for kicks.

But something else was in the works. In my desert experience at college I sought counsel. A wonderful professor of sociology, who had studied theology also, had lent me his ear and hours of listening. He hinted that my experience might have been an indication to consider the Christian ministry rather than law as a life's calling. I hesitated because I had dodged baptism three times. The water seemed irrelevant and inconvenient. The symbolism had not been made clear.

One Sunday morning I got up early, walked two and a half miles off campus to a Baptist church, heard a moving sermon, and submitted myself for baptism. The theme of that sermon was God's words to Joshua: "As I was with Moses, so I will be with thee: I will not fail thee, nor forsake thee. [Therefore,] be strong and of a good courage; be not afraid, neither be thou dismayed: for the LORD thy God is with thee whithersoever thou goest" (Joshua 1:5,9). That did it.

So eighteen years old, tall, thin, curious, confused, with two years of college behind me and a lifetime ahead, I went into the navy yard every day; and I let the playboy and the preacher bid for my soul. Meanwhile, my childhood affection for the church caused me to be there every Sunday. And the relevant sermons of the Reverend D.C. Rice, a bright, warm-hearted, clear-thinking, concerned pastor, and his enthusiasm for the Christian message caused the playboy image to seem less and less satisfying and the image of the servant of Christ in his church to be harder and harder to reject.

The problem I did not have was that of finding my freedom. I had found it and had used it. So once I made my decision, I went to the labor board, resigned my apprenticeship, bought some books, took a job that relieved the pressure, drew closer to my wonderful pastor, canvassed new college options, and pursued my new calling. My friends found it hard to take me as a preacher, putting down my alto saxophone and our jazz combo, giving up a secure future as a well-paid master shipfit-ter for the navy, and entering a long period of study with no guarantee of employment or success. But I had found my freedom and used it.

Concerning our freedom, perhaps the most crucial use of freedom is the long reach into our future that we make when we commit our lives to a life's work, such as teaching, preach-ing, medicine, military service, or the performing arts—to a career calling for a heavy investment of preparation and a long risk. In 1940 I made the commitment to the work of the church, and when I returned to college, I was serious about it.

Freedom includes freedom to fail, freedom to choose to quit, freedom to be turned around, and freedom to look for the resources to remain steadfast. The first challenge came when the college I chose rejected my music credits; though I had been a full junior, I was reduced to a second-semester freshman. To a nineteen-year-old working his way through school, that was a test! But the night following that discovery, I began a practice of going into prayer, learning to live a life of trust, reaching beyond the facts and the hard data and letting life remain suspended on the surmise that God was real and responsive to my earnest prayers.

I found the strength to go on, and by piling up courses and

taking maximum loads, I not only graduated in two years and a summer, but I did it mostly with A's. And I loved it. As I *used* my freedom, I felt it *grow*. Discipline and toughness were the immediate rewards.

At Virginia Union, a Baptist college founded by the white Baptists of the North following the Civil War to train black ministers, I found a liberal arts atmosphere enriched by a handful of truly great teachers. Arthur W. Davis had a fresh Ph.D. from Columbia in English literature, with a dissertation on Isaac Watts; Mary E. Johnson was recently returned with her doctorate in French literature from the Sorbonne; Henry J. McGuin had a new sociology Ph.D. under the venerated Professor MacIver of Columbia; Limas D. Wall had a doctorate in biology from Michigan; and Richard I. McKinney had a Ph.D. in philosophy of religion from Yale. Our president, John M. Ellison, was a Drew Ph.D. I name them because I wish to make the point that no matter how large or small a school may be, it really takes only five or six devoted professors to cause one to be introduced to the life of the mind and to enter the world of thought and reflection. One may roam through the canyons of schools one hundred times larger and never find a professor whose concern will result in a true intellectual emancipation.

Our universities are free, without rigid controls, and we trust this atmosphere of academic freedom to deliver a stream of truly bright and creative minds. But if the campus is polluted by a "country club" atmosphere, if professors are preoccupied with gaining a "name" from research and despise teaching, and if no sense of true purpose can be felt, the freedom granted the academic community is a waste and an abuse of the school's benefactions.

We were made alive to current issues as well as to the cultural and political antecedents to our situation. And on a small campus the possibility for close relationship and meaningful interchange was real. We knew everyone on campus. Also, without much money, with no student center, no parties with "kegs" of beer, no legal abortions, no credit cards, no Toyotas or Corvettes or Mustangs, we had to be creative. I recall that our student government association observed that the famous orchestra of Fred Waring and his Pennsylvanians would present on radio every Saturday morning the school songs of the big universities: Wisconsin, Notre Dame, Illinois, Penn State, and so forth. We decided to wire him a request to play our song, from a small, black, Baptist college in Virginia. He wired back immediately that he would. We scurried around, found the music, acquired copyright clearances, and so forth, and connected a dozen radios by extension cords hanging from dormitory windows. All of us stood in a huge circle arm in arm and cried shamelessly as we heard our song played for the whole country by the wonderful Fred Waring band. One thing after another confirmed how real freedom was.

While at home for Christmas in 1941, I worked my favorite job: running the elevators in our brand-new department store. The uniforms were elegant and the people extremely pleasant. One day a porter passed my elevator and teased me: "Reverend, go the hell on up. Nobody wants to ride up with a preacher." (When I had worked there earlier, he delighted in teasing me about wanting to be a minister.) An elderly, deep-voiced, highly regarded white pastor of the leading church in town heard him. He came toward me as I stood by my elevator. "Did he call you a preacher?" he asked. "Yes, sir." "Are you one?" he continued. "Yes, sir. I am in college, planning to go to the seminary next September." "Which one?" he asked. "I have not decided. I will need a scholarship; so I'll have to wait and see where I can get some help."

It turned out that he was a trustee of Crozer, and he asked me to contact him if I wanted to consider his school. I did, and I was awarded a scholarship. This pastor gave me boxes of books and continued to inquire about my well-being. He was the town's high priest and prophet, a town completely segregated and loyal to all the canons of racial separation and discrimination that prevailed. But we all had a tacit understanding that personal kindnesses and concerns were allowed to penetrate the segregation wall. The implication was that in private matters one may treat persons as individuals, but in civil matters one had to maintain a wall of separation. There was also a tacit assumption that it was a matter of time when the personal relations would erode the social practice, but no one rushed it.

At Crozer I faced another test of my choice—to leave home and go North—and my freedom was challenged the first day. There I was up North, and when the student jobs were assigned, I—the only "colored" in the whole school—was assigned to wash the pots and pans and scrub the kitchen floor. There I was, with a tuition scholarship from a famous white pastor, excellent academic record, one of the few with two years of classical Greek—mopping the kitchen every night at midnight.

The simple fact was that even seminary professors, who made the assignments, had not thought critically about racial customs, and it was easy for them to do the expected thing and send the "colored" boy to the kitchen. I was shocked and humiliated, but I had learned not to succumb to instinctive responses but to live above them and to impose on my impulses my value scale. My freedom conferred upon me the privilege of looking at the situation objectively. So I turned that kitchen into a temple like the one Isaiah saw filled with smoke; it became my Patmos where I envisioned my new Jerusalem, my Midian desert where my bush was on fire. I sang and prayed and preached to myself while scrubbing the floor, all the while gaining the strength to face that and any other obstacle with firmness and high resolution.

The compensating experience was the way my fellow students, practically all of whom had come from the South, underwent their social metamorphosis and accepted me warmly. One of them, Rabon Rose from North Carolina, threatened to whip me if he caught me downtown getting a haircut at the "colored" barber shop. He demanded that I, a black from Virginia and our segregated barber shops, allow him, a white from North Carolina, to be my barber. I did. And he was.

The ultimate test of my freedom was the challenge to view the Bible differently. I was bound intellectually and spiritually, by loyalty to tradition and by emotional satisfaction, to cling to the Bible as the literal, inerrant word of God without further debate. But my college education had prepared me for inquiry at any level into anything. What, then, would I do when I discovered that the Bible was not one book but sixty-six that had existed as separate documents until canonized in the fourth century, three hundred years after Jesus' death? How would I take finding out that several other books had been candidates for the canon but were rejected by vote of the church, not by a bolt of lightning or a voice from heaven?

Well, it was during my first year that my sacred Bible was subjected to assaults from all corners: (1) the physical sciences offered a different view of the origin, shape, and destiny of planet earth and the entire solar systems—with evidence of other suns beyond our own; (2) the study of anthropology and the history of other cultures challenged the Jews' claims on being *the* chosen people and Abraham being *the* father of the faithful; and (3) the study of the language and the timetables of the Bible itself laid open the possibility that the whole book had to be rearranged chronologically, with Amos and Micah the oldest writings; the Hebrew stories of creation, the flood, and so forth, written at about the fourth century B.C.; Ezra and Nehemiah written after the sixth-century Jewish captivity in Babylon, followed by Ruth and Jonah to counter the new ethnic narrowness found in Ezra and Nehemiah; and these followed by the great *hero* and *heroine* literature of Daniel and Esther.

It was painful to have to consider Job simply as an inspired, philosophical poem depicting the enduring faithfulness of a devout servant of God despite his enormous losses and inscrutable, undeserved suffering. Additional pain came from learning that a scribe would not *leave* Job as the valiant, spiritual genius that he was, but had to cheapen the quality of Job's faith by *rewarding* him with the return of his health and all things, double! We were taught that Job was not a lesson in how to regain losses by being faithful but how to be faithful *anyhow*, losses regained or not!

In the New Testament we had to face the fact that neither Mark's, John's, nor Paul's writings mentioned the virgin birth of Jesus and that Paul spoke of the resurrection in spiritual terms. In the end, we had to understand that the Bible did not create God, Jesus, or the Holy Spirit in the church. These were all *realities* before a *single line* was written by anyone. The Bible is a *record* of the events, not the events themselves, and the recording of the events was a process subject to human fallibility and human perceptions. But God is real, Jesus lived and the Christ of faith lives still, and the Holy Spirit is here, both then and now. So high religion seeks *to relate* one to the *living* God about whom the Bible speaks, *to know* the Jesus of the Judean hills and the Jericho road, and *to experience* within oneself the fire of the Holy Spirit that the book of Acts talks about. This meant that one was allowed to study the written documents themselves with all of the honest inquiry, the diligence, the scrutiny, the enlightenment that one could command. Such study could only lead to a richer, purer knowledge of God and a deeper, more loving loyalty to the Christ about whom the New Testament exploded.

In order to get through it all, I leaned heavily on the sermons and writings of Harry Emerson Fosdick. He did not run from the new insights or from the political threats hurled by so-called defenders of the Word. He let the light of history, science, physics, archaeology, and psychology come shining through. I ended up with a Bible better understood and a warmer faith in that God who was the source of *all* truth, from wherever. And I found Jesus more real; with a more lasting trust and devotion he was my Savior.

4

DEVELOPING
a Well-Equipped Conscience

INTRODUCTION TO CONSCIENCE
FROM SEMINARY

Many persons have no idea of what happens in a theological seminary. Apparently, some think that we sit around and memorize Bible verses and practice preaching at one another. All seminary enrollees have completed an accredited college course somewhere, and the majors vary widely. All the professors have earned doctoral degrees or have long and esteemed experience in some areas of church endeavor. It is a serious and demanding three-year program. The purpose is to give each student a thorough understanding of the spiritual experiences and the religious community out of which the Bible came; to learn the history of the Christian church and its relationship to the cultures and institutions with which it interrelated; to examine the human psyche—its makeup and its needs; to analyze the social, political, and economic composition of the society where the gospel will be preached and the struggle engaged in to cause the kingdom of God to "come on earth as it is in heaven."

Then one is taught the skills and appropriate strategies to keep the church vital, relevant, and thriving. The agenda that lies parallel to all of this is that each student will be growing in earnestness, piety, and moral integrity so that she or he will become an answer, not another problem, in representing the cause of Christ in the world.

So the net effect should be that upon graduation this whole experience of academic study, worship, and prayer will result in each graduate having a Christian conscience, the mind of Christ, and the discipline to be trusted to lead the people. Moreover, not only should this happen within the students, but their purpose should be to go out into society, working in and through the churches, to cause the people to become initiated also into the mind of Christ and a Christian conscience.

How well all of that happens is the ultimate test; in 1945 I was ushered out of the seminary, and the test began. It was not easy to assure that my own conscience was well enough equipped in 1945—or in 1989, 44 years later! And the assurance is still tinged with great doubt. But the real world is out there as a moral frontier waiting for the insights, the encouragement, the life-changing ministrations of those prepared by training, example, and their serious commitment.

Recently, at Abyssinian Church in New York City, an elderly deacon arrived late for a service at which he was usually the first one present. As he found his seat, he was noticeably out of breath and trembling. His face was pale with fear. While daylight was slowly fading before nightfall, he had started out of his home from a neat, respectable apartment building. As he reached the sidewalk, he came upon a teenage drug dealer holding a gun to the forehead of another teenager, a "pusher," demanding his money. The deacon said that he heard the young pusher plead for the dealer to wait a few minutes more until another pusher would show up with the money. But the dealer would not wait. His black BMW was parked at the curb, windows painted, with the motor running; he had on his leather jacket, his gold chains, rings, and bracelets, and the gun was cocked menacingly. The deacon fled back into his building's vestibule and heard the crack of gunfire. The young pusher gave up his whole future as he lay dying on the sidewalk.

Beginning with this awful scene and working our way around it, we find it to be a sad and tragic pivotal point; and as we work our way around it, we see what a circle of moral decay surrounds us. We become aware instantly of our pathetic inability to find an answer to such horror. Next, we recognize that if something is not done soon, the total fabric of society will be ripped apart. Furthermore, we grieve that our nation—possessing such magic technology, such abundant wealth, such an enviable standard of living, such high and noble promises drafted into its Declaration of Independence and its Preamble to the Constitution, and embracing the Bible within the preponderant Judeo-Christian institutions— could reach the moral crisis that now threatens us. Yet the crisis is about much more than brutal and robotized young drug dealers, heavily armed, in the urban canyons. It is also about preserving in our children a sense of moral earnestness and a commitment to moral responsibility.

My two younger sons, Steven and Sam, spent two entire summers gripped by curiosity and caught in a strange silence, watching the Watergate hearings on television; and as they have grown older, they have become numb to the continuous revelations of moral failure throughout the society; frequent reports of malfeasance in city, state, and federal government; police bribery; corporate cheating; Pentagon and Wall Street fraud disclosures; and the shocking, secret Irangate "government" in the White House basement. The spread of AIDS; the drug epidemic; new urban racial confrontations; and the rising divorce, abortion, child abuse, and crime rates all point to a serious need for moral recovery.

Moreover, the social and cultural atmosphere is not in our favor, with a serious weakening of the family, a discipline crisis in our schools, a wave of "privatization" and personal success moving among our "brightest" and our "best," a "soap opera" social outlook guiding our moral understanding, and a cold, widespread contempt for the powerless and the poor dominating the national mood.

OUR LOCUS OF CONTROL

There is such a thing as learning and recognizing where the control of one's life is really coming from: are my peers dictating what I wear, the car I drive, what I do, where I spend vacations, and the church I attend? Are persons in my family controlling me like a puppet on a string? Does my boss make all my choices? Do my club members? My neighbors, my children, my spouse? Or do I keep secure and inviolate a chamber of choice within me? And if such a sacred chamber does exist, how is it furnished? Indeed, our locus of control should be within us, and in moral terms we call it conscience. At the age of independence and responsibility one becomes aware of the necessity of having a well-equipped conscience.

It is one thing to know about the locus of control, but it is another actually to be out there on one's own, flying on "automatic pilot." Decisions have to be made fast, firmly, and finally, and the very best preparation is to have a well-equipped conscience.

In 1945 I was twenty-four years old but really acting much older. I had been married to a college schoolmate, Bessie Tate from Fredericksburg, Virginia, for a full year, while completing my seminary work. We had very little money and worried hardly at all about things. We had each other. In my senior year we had the added benefit of living in the home of the seminary president, where we helped with household chores in exchange for room and board and a few dollars extra. The president was a brilliant, highly reputed theologian and his wife a prominent civic leader. In addition, I managed the small campus bookstore. I cannot imagine where I found the energy, but my ambition made a machine out of me.

Somehow, even though I had been admitted for a Yale Ph.D. program and had won the coveted Crozer Fellowship, I hungered for a preaching assignment. One was offered, and the plan was to live and preach in a small parish in Providence and commute weekly to New Haven. Of course, after one year

I had to revert to plan "B" and defer graduate study. Our family began, and everything had to be adjusted.

All of these decisions and responsibilities as pastor, husband, father-to-be, young scholar, and community leader found me a long way from professors, away from the intense fellowship of seminary buddies, away from my own pastor, my daddy, my mother, and my mother-in-law (who was as close as a mother)—and a long way from home. There I was on "automatic pilot"; I was in flight, and my guide was that sacred chamber within that sounded off with applause for right choices and with wailing and groaning for wrong or questionable ones. All earlier authority symbols were suddenly removed. Grown, married, and a long way from home, I leaned on that locus of control from within called conscience.

CONSCIENCE AS A
SIXTH SENSE

Of all the trials and burdens of early adulthood, the most troubling *is* the discovery that even though a person is grown and free to do whatever he or she wants to do, there is a quiet restraint that monitors one's behavior from within. It is like a moral barometer, and just as the weather barometer responds to atmospheric pressures, this moral monitor measures the pressures pushing against the moral sensitivities. This is why it has been thought of as a sixth sense, but it is commonly called "conscience."

One of the monumental philosophical theorists was the seventeenth-century Dutch thinker Benedict Spinoza. He was so completely committed to the life of the mind that he seemed to have heard some rumblings out of eternity inaudible to the rest of us. In his *Ethics,* published after his death, he talked about conscience. He believed that conscience was acquired, not an innate, given "sixth sense." He saw it as a social invention, the repository of the moral values and traditions of one's group. While conscience was not given naturally—but earned and developed—it was still the efficient means by which the society protected itself from raw, untamed human nature and its unhoned, selfish, agressive propensities.

Emerging out of the seminary with my wife of one year and taking off for a new life as a young pastor, and a graduate student, I was truly on my own. But, as Spinoza pointed out, I was loaded with a loyalty to those principles, values, traditions, and behavior patterns that I had learned in Huntersville. It was more than memory; it was loyalty, buttressed by love and gratitude. I wanted to be approved by Mrs. Billups, Mrs. Epps, Mrs. Mary Williams, Miss Constance Fuller, Mr. Eugene West, Mr. G. W. C. Brown, and Reverend Henderson. Most of all, I wanted Grandma, Aunt Nannie, Mamma, and Daddy to be proud. I wanted my mother-in-law, Stella Hill Tate, to feel good about her daughter's life with me. Conscience was strong, in shape, and real.

In me was a catalog of things to say and never to say; to do and not ever to think of doing; places to be and places not ever to be found, even dead! Any thought of violating those taboos brought on stomach disorders, dizziness, and black dots before my eyes! In addition to that jury back in Huntersville, there was that long and satisfying friendship with Jesus, my Savior and Lord. Despite my rigorous, challenging New Testament studies and all the inquiries into the accuracy of the data of the Gospels, in my heart there was that basic, unquestioned allegiance to the Jesus of Galilee, which was another powerful restraint.

So much for the *content* of my conscience. What of the *binding quality*, the agglutinating force? Why was it so painful to veto conscience, to turn off the alarm, to lower the volume? Whenever I did such a thing, the alarm system worked all too well, and the guilt was consuming.

Immanuel Kant, the eighteenth-century German idealist, helps us with his insight also. In his treatise "Critique of Practical Reason" he argued that we were equipped with an *absolute moral sense* and that the mind was not a moral *tabula rasa*, or clean tablet. He gave us a principle called the "categorical imperative": ". . . act as if the maxim of our action were to become by our will a universal law of nature." In other words, we are endowed with a moral sense that whispers, "Let your conduct be such that if *everyone* did what you do, you would still be satisfied." (This is a very loose paraphrase.)

I never felt the need to choose between the views of Spinoza and Kant on whether conscience was acquired socially or given naturally. Granted, it is a functioning, active repository of accumulated loyalties, and it does bind. The main question is what those loyalties are to which Spinoza refers and this *moral sense* of Kant's that binds us so effectively. Conscience does work, whether we are given it by nature (Kant) or acquire it through society (Spinoza).

The apostle Paul warned us not to be conformed to this world, but to be transformed by the renewal of the mind. He taught that in Christ we would become new creations. So from the Christian perspective, these loyalties and sentiments that comprise our conscience are subject to review against the teachings and example of Jesus, and whatever may be the natural moral sense that Kant spoke of is now given over to a new moral commitment to Jesus Christ.

Therefore, one could see two people standing side by side, both speaking and behaving in much the same way. But one is acting out those loyalties fixed in childhood and acquired in good schooling, and is bound by that moral sense that Kant said all humans possessed. The other, acting much the same way, is responding in obedience to Jesus and bound by the love of Christ from within. And the apparent similarities in behavior may last a long time, but eventually there would come the moment when the radical teachings of Jesus would differ distinctly from those acquired values that the society generated out of trial and error and had settled down as mere custom. Jesus goes further. He taught that if our enemy hungered, we should feed him; if he thirsted, give him drink. He taught us to forgive seventy-times seven times. He said that whoever would be greatest among us should be servant of all.

These behavior patterns would hardly be a part of that "conscience" put together by the normal observations of human behavior. Jesus goes further. And speaking of binding, perseverance, and loyalty, Jesus adds much to whatever nature requires. He said that we should deny ourselves, take up our cross, and follow him.

CONSCIENCE AND RELIGION

The apostle Paul takes us deeply into his confidence in the epistle to the Philippians and lays out before us how his conscience was put together. After all, before his conversion he helped to have Christians killed. In Acts 7:58 we find Paul participating in the stoning of Stephen, the first person named a deacon in the young church. Paul's name was Saul then. And throughout his preaching career he was bold to explain how clean his conscience was, for he saw himself as a defender of the faith of his fathers. In Philippians 3:4–6 he gives us his pedigree: of the stock of Israel, tribe of Benjamin, Hebrew, and Pharisee. Then he says, "Concerning zeal, persecuting the church; touching the righteousness which is in the law, blameless." He felt right in what he was doing. His religion sanctioned all of it.

What makes religion so very important with respect to conscience is that it does represent our highest loyalty. Our strongest commitments are to whatever we regard as ultimate, and for most of us it is our religious faith. We make high promises at moments of solemn reflection, while the great organ and the choral refrains reinforce our resolve with emotional appeals for loyalty and dedication. So if our religious beliefs are inadequate to furnish our conscience, we find ourselves doing wrong with great sincerity.

Recently, on a television talk show appeared a man in his mid-forties with two of his wives, a woman and her teenage daughter, both married to him! The daughter had been only fifteen when he married her. There were two other wives at home who could not make the show. He argued that his religion allowed him to have four wives. They all obeyed him and alternated on a four-night schedule in sharing his bed with him. Amazing what religion will allow the conscience to approve if the religious concepts are morally flawed in the first place!

One of the most troublesome aspects of dissolving apartheid in South Africa is that the strongest church in that distressed land has endorsed and embraced the concept for so many generations. The consciences of people have sounded no alarms. On the other hand, John Brown's conscience was equipped with other ideas and loyalties stemming from his religious beliefs; and on October 16, 1859, he led an army of twenty-two ardent abolitionists to seize the federal armory at Harper's Ferry. For this he paid with his life and the lives of two sons. So when one says that his or her conscience is equipped and fueled and illumined by his or her religion, we need to know, then, what kind of religion it is. Indeed, religion does have this binding quality, but bound to what?

As a young pastor in 1945 I was curious to discover what it was that religious persons felt obliged to do in the name of conscience. And, indeed, I was humbled by what I felt conscientious about as the new young shepherd right out of the seminary. As I reflect upon it now, I regret that I did not lead the members of the church more faithfully into a closer discipleship to Jesus but, instead, led them into a larger brick edifice, with more middle-class people enjoying the sentiments of religiosity and each other's fellowship but too largely with only passing interest in a sustained fellowship with God.

Religion is not simply one option among many; it is, rather, the foundation of the integrity, wholeness, and completeness of any life. It raises for us those broad and all-encompassing questions from which the smaller, everyday questions spring. And when those big questions are answered adequately, satisfactorily, earnestly, and convincingly, such answers comprise the faith and belief system that answers all subordinate questions about life and its moral ambiguities. Conscience, then, is not fully equipped until religion has had its say; until we have settled on the big questions about the meaning and purpose of life, the quality of our relationship with others, the range and scope of our highest loyalties, and our notion about how all of this gets wrapped up and reaches a solemn conclusion one day. And it is not enough to make a cold decision and stop there. No. In order for religion to function as the center of a good and alert conscience, religion must be alive and verdant and nurtured by worship and celebration.

In the July 4–11, 1984, issue of *The Christian Century* there appeared a reprinting of a November 6, 1919, article by Harry Emerson Fosdick. It meant so much to me because when I had reached my senior year in seminary, I had wondered if I would give up the preaching ministry altogether and teach sociology or become a full-time peace advocate. Evangelical Christianity ran a slow third because my Bible had been ripped apart by historical and literary criticism; my Huntersville God-idea had been shattered by naturalism and humanism, and while Jesus was left, his image was "battle weary," too. I had nothing to go and preach about! So the struggle was for my very soul and the spiritual integrity of my life.

On his weekly radio programs Dr. Fosdick went after persons just like me. There was nothing superficial or simpleminded about his message. He was dead serious, and he probed into my doubts with penetrating thoroughness. He swept every corner of doubt and confusion clean with wide, strong strokes from the witness of literature, history, biology, astronomy, and the Bible. But this Bible of his was more about the living God who *caused* it to be written, more about the character and victory of Jesus who was its main subject, and more about the vitality of the Holy Spirit than it was about literal inerrancy and plenary infallibility. He never debated those hair-splitting biblical issues, but like a big ship headed out to sea he followed the deep-water channels of truth into real salvation and everlasting life! So his ministry brought me home, *never* more to roam. For some he was a mischievous "liberal." For me he was a great shepherd of those students who were once lost but now were found. From the majestic pulpit of the incomparable, inimitable Riverside Church, his voice reached countless wandering minds and restored for them a warm, personal faith in God and an honest conviction about the unique divinity of the Preacher from Galilee. I would testify, therefore, that talk about conscience is not over until we talk about a sense of God's reality. And that is what Fosdick's 1919 article was all about, and why it was reissued seventy-five years later.

When conscience is asked to respond to the complicated questions that are hurled at it today, it is no wonder that it sputters and flutters, fizzes and fumes, blows and pants, and gives with a warbly, muffled uncertain sound. Conscience is too frail and fragile without a firm God-concept at its center, a concept that effuses radiance and light for shadowy and blurred moral dilemmas.

Faith in God addresses such issues as what life is worth and how precious each passing moment is. Faith in God reminds us of how important all persons are in God's sight. Faith in God assures us that truth and righteousness have some reliable sponsorship and that they shall prevail in the end. Faith in God guarantees to us that nothing good that we do will be lost but will become another atom in a universe of love. Faith in God calls us to serve those who need us most, to empower those with no power at all, to protect those without any defense; and it causes us to walk on high places and to shine as stars in the night as we live in the forgiving and sustaining love and grace of God.

Not only an intellectual decision about God gives life to the conscience, but a lively awareness of the reality of God does as well. Those who have known real moral fatigue and failure—and how poorly we function when the conscience is void of God—will recognize what the prophet to the exiles was describing:

> . . . they who wait for the LORD shall renew their
> strength,
> they shall mount up with wings like eagles,

they shall run and not be weary,
they shall walk and not faint.
—Isaiah 40:31, RSV

From this moral energy comes a well-equipped conscience, with active signals and clear directions for crisp and decisive moral choices.

CONSCIENCE AND THE ISSUES
OF SOCIETY

A well-equipped, finely tuned, alert, and sensitized conscience will respond when it is violated in matters of personal behavior, but it will respond equally as sharply in matters of social failure and injustice. During the period following my seminary days, when the world was repairing itself from the bludgeoning and harrowing of World War II, there was a new conscience emerging as we learned more about the horrors of the genocide of the Jews, the extreme poverty of places like Calcutta, the ugly racism of South Africa, and the quiet, polite racism in America that indulged complete separation of races in schools, labor unions, concert halls, libraries, churches, and graveyards. The new world that we prayed for seemed to be incongruous with this colonialism, racism, and severe economic disparity. All the idealistic notions about which I had written term papers in seminary were crying out for application. The words yearned to become flesh.

Everything that happened seemed to resonate in octaves. The American Baptists opened their new conference site at Green Lake, Wisconsin, in 1947 with a small group of concerned pastors dealing with Christian social concern. Three of us from Rhode Island drove across the scenic mountains and the verdant plains to Green Lake. Reaching Detroit late at night, we called the YMCA for lodging. When we appeared to register, a crippled night attendant, hobbling on a cane, shouted at me that no "colored" could stay at the YMCA. My companions, John Zuber and Artemis Goodwin, were two

77

wonderful white pastors. They and I left in quiet resignation and went to the "colored" Young Men's Christian Association to spend the night. We represented genuine community traveling together, and we confronted denial of community at the Young Men's Christian Association. You can imagine the main topic for discussion when we arrived at the conference on Christian Social Concern led by Donald Cloward, the social conscience of the Baptists, with a few others.

This alerted conscience in social matters often caused troubling dilemmas when applied. One day I drove past the stately Roman Catholic cathedral on the main artery through town, a few short blocks from our small church. There, spread out on the wide marble steps of the cathedral was a 240-pound priest, thoroughly inebriated, drooling at the mouth and gazing at the sky aimlessly. I paused at the curb. Conscience had summoned me, but I did not know what to do.

I knew the bishop and several of the priests there, and knocking on all doors at dusk drew no response. Should I call the police, call another Catholic church, leave him there to be discovered by someone in the parish, get a friend to move him—where? I hastened home and did call a friendly police sergeant, who was understanding. Conscience had sounded off, but in a society of confused protocol the choices were not so clear.

After serving for four years and being taught so much by a patient, loving, long-suffering congregation, and with some experience on the local Urban League board of directors, I realized the time had come to return to the South and to begin the task of teaching in a seminary, my first love. I had learned much from graduate study at Yale and Boston University and from association with Reverend and Mrs. Kenneth Cober of the Rhode Island Baptist Convention and the larger circle of pastors of all denominations serving in Providence at the time. One could not hope to be in fellowship with any finer group of pastors. I honestly feared how I would thrive returning to the South, which resisted change so adamantly.

However, with my conscience having been tuned to be open

and ecumenical and having been sensitized to hope for the best from all persons, I came to the South without a chip on my shoulder. What *was* on my shoulder was our two-and-a-half-year-old son, born with an open valve between the ventricles of his heart that should have closed at birth. It was tetralogy of Fallot, more commonly called "blue baby." He needed a surgical procedure not yet devised, and his life's chances without it were practically nil. We needed more money, warm friends, a lot of faith, and a rapid development in open-heart surgery. Waiting was wearing, and hope was dim.

We learned through the press and gossip that a renowned cardiologist was in Richmond, where we lived, and that he taught at the Medical College of Virginia. He was also an heir to a large, wealthy Virginia family from one of the most conservative sections of the state, near the place where Nat Turner, a slave insurrectionist, had killed dozens of slave owners in 1859. Would I dare go to him with my little boy's defective heart?

The fact was that I knew that I was beyond categorizing persons on the basis of race or origin. Surely I was apprehensive, but nothing in my heart had concluded that this cardiologist, Dr. Paul Camp, would resent our visit. My wife and I went. This was one more exploration on our part in search of a ray of hope, and the result had been that we were better rehearsed at praying and were drawn more closely together by virtue of this extra bond of desperation.

Dr. Camp, a big man with a boy's face, reached for our little fellow as though he had been waiting for him a long time. And in minutes this wealthy, celebrated cardiologist from Virginia's "bluebloods" held our boy in one arm and the telephone with the other. He was talking with the children's heart specialist at Johns Hopkins in Baltimore and arranging for Dr. Helen Taussig to see our son within days and to begin to work him up for surgery. (Today our son is a school social worker, the father of three fine children, bowling over two hundred, and singing bass in the North Jersey Philarmonic

Glee Club! Two heart corrections at Johns Hopkins gave him a normal life. Those miracles had begun in the arms of a white cardiologist in Richmond while my wife and I had trembled with the suspicion that the world had not changed that much.)

This moral barometer inside of us, a composite of our values, our affections and devotion, and our solid commitments, is not put together once and for all time. It is subject to review and repair. And none of this is sudden, like an ice cube dropped in a glass or paint stroked on a wall. In fact, it is more like the greening of the leaves in springtime or a baby learning to walk. It has a required process. And in that segment of time from seminary to a position of much broader responsibility, I saw the conscience that I brought from my youth undergo a series of revisions and modifications. No doubt, the most serious change was to bring my view of society and the world under the same close scrutiny that I had applied to matters of personal behavior. It takes time for us to understand how Jesus placed relationship to God in tandem to relationship to the least of these our brothers and sisters.

GIVING OUR CONSCIENCE
AN APPRAISAL

The May 25, 1987, issue of *Time* magazine presented a gallery of sixty outstanding persons from government, business, the military, hi-tech, and "media-savvy" evangelism who had either been accused, indicted, convicted, or driven out of positions of trust because of violation of the law or failure to meet those minimum standards of morality that are generally accepted in this society. These were current events, items in the news at the time of publication or within weeks prior. It was no year-long accumulation. They were high-rolling stockbrokers, trusted White House aides, a front-running presidential candidate, a decorated Marine sargent, cabinet-level officials, an air force major, bank executives, corporation CEOs, and a world-famous producer of name-brand fashions. The list omitted professional ball players suspended for drug use or congressmen arrested for drunk driving.

The fact is that those presented were merely the ones exposed. Most persons believe that beneath this tip there is an iceberg, and these persons only reflect a deep moral pathology that troubles our land.

Among these persons are those who used public monies for private gains; government leaders who told slimy ethnic jokes; corporate heads who cheated in billing the government; persons who sold military secrets; others who violated marriage vows; more who stole public property, cheated on tax returns, received bribes, lied under oath, and beat their wives.

Beneath much of this failure was the lust for money and a disregard for the level of trust that the public had ascribed to these persons and their positions. As one looks at them and their excellent educational and favored economic backgrounds, the privileged status they enjoyed, the high earnings they commanded, one wonders what went wrong. Why did not their consciences sound a warning, flash lights, blow a whistle, or lower the temperature? What kind of conscience had one cultivated that functioned so poorly and that slept through such temptations?

Conscience will guide us. Conscience *does* guide us. But what is the moral quality, the equipment, the value system that the conscience contains?

As I pondered questions about morality and purpose in living, I was brought with an uncommon seriousness to the issue—not only from my classes with Liston Pope, Richard Niebuhr, and Roland Bainton at Yale and Robert Pfeiffer and Edwin Booth at Boston University, but from a sharpened focus developed by looking into my son's eyes and considering his future and his needs. Weighing life's meaning was no longer an academic hobby. It was real. And as a young pastor I had to deal with the criteria for examining conscience and revitalizing it. This is the kind of material that creeps into sermons without labels, questions such as "What are the real basics of moral judgment? When have I done wrong? Am I to accept teachings from ancient Judaism or first-century Christianity as final for the modern world? If I really wanted to refine my conscience, what should I be saying to myself?"

There are those who say that behavior is good when it brings maximum pleasure with the least pain; others say behavior is good when it promotes the greatest good for the greatest number; others say that behavior is good when it is in harmony with nature and avoids extremes of any kind; others say that behavior is good when it promotes the survival of the fittest and eliminates weakness and dependency; others say it is good when it promotes self-realization, when it is obedient to Scripture, when it obeys the law, or when it is guided by the Holy Spirit. These are the issues that I wrestled with as a young pastor and a doctoral student, preparing to teach ethics and religion in college.

I found that many persons were quick to say that a good conscience required behavior in obedience to the Bible, but they hardly knew what it meant to say that. They really meant the Ten Commandments; the sublime teachings of Amos, Micah, and Isaiah; and the example in word and deed of Jesus. They did not mean to copy the behavior of Lot, who, having drunk so much wine, was not aware of impregnating both of his daughters; or to obey Paul when he counseled slaves to obey their masters or to follow his counsel to remain unmarried, as it was; or to have as many wives as David and Solomon had; or to be as unforgiving as Esther, Nehemiah, and Ezra had been; or to be as brutal as Saul was in requiring David to kill two hundred Philistines in order to present their foreskins as a dowry for Saul's daughter Michal.

Hardly did they mean any of that. The Bible is not consistent in the morality that it presents. It did not intend to be. We have imposed that idea on the Bible. It is sixty-six books written over a span of one thousand years, at least, by different authors, with differing audiences, and for different purposes. God speaks to us through the Bible as inspired characters bear God's revealed message to us. But not every character of the Bible bears such a message, and some who do, like Paul, do not do so all the time. He said so himself in 1 Corinthians 7:25!

The Christians that I know who represent the finest of moral tone and example and whose lives are a benediction to us all are trying to walk in the footsteps of Jesus. And, indeed, it is the Bible that brings the life and teachings of Jesus to us.

On the other hand, we have always been challenged by those who prefer to inform their consciences to seek the greatest happiness with the least concomitant pain. However, this approach does not account for the numberless saints and martyrs, like old Polycarp, who endured the most indescribable pain in order *to be pleased* to obey Christ; or Harriet Tubman, who led hundreds of slaves to freedom while she was sick, wading through swamps in pitch darkness and hiding in mountain clefts. It was not *her own* pleasure but the freedom of slaves that she sought. Indeed, the morality of many goes no further than pleasure, and they always remain indebted to others whose morality is more substantial.

The greatest good for the greatest number sounds good until someone argues that killing Jews seemed to be a greater good for the majority in Germany in the 1940s or that holding black slaves was a greater good for the greater number of whites in America for 247 years. No. We must find out what the greatest good is, first, before we declare it valid for the greater—or even the lesser—number.

Cooperation with and obedience to nature seem innocent enough as a moral guide except that good medicinal practice, improved agriculture, longer life, lower blood pressure, flood control, and vaccines against killer diseases were all the results of a *veto over and a contest with* nature! In fact, we make a habit of making nature serve our higher values rather than bowing to nature's caprice. Nature's power and resources are put to those uses that *our* values determine. Only the weakest among us live in blind response to nature's whim.

Morality based upon obedience to the law is good if the laws are good. For one hundred years we had laws that discriminated against women and blacks; obviously, a higher morality than obedience to such unjust laws was required.

Morality based on obedience to the Holy Spirit cannot be any higher, provided it *is* the Holy Spirit that one is obeying. The content of obedience needs to be tested somehow. Reverend Jim Jones of California was led by the "spirit" to cause hundreds of followers to die of poison, and the Mormons were led by the "spirit" to deny blacks priesthood because of race until very recently. Indeed, *if* it is God's Holy Spirit and *if* it conforms to God's revelation in Jesus, no higher moral direction could be found.

One finds that in the example of Jesus Christ are a moral guide and a criterion for a good conscience that incorporate the best in all of these other positions. There is respect and gratitude for all that God provides through nature's endowments. There is concern for pleasure, but it is a pleasure that is found in right relationship to God. This pleasure may indeed call for sacrifice and pain, but the pain results in pleasing God, our highest good. In Christ we search for the greatest good first, and then we try to share it with all, the greatest number. In Jesus there is self-realization, but it begins not with seeking our own good but the good of others. Our realized selves are achieved as we seek the realized self in others. "Whosoever shall seek to save his life shall lose it; and whosoever shall lose his life shall preserve it" (Luke 17:33).

The person whose conscience is equipped to imitate Christ finds that this imitation is not so much a philosophy or calculated code of conduct as it is a relationship, a loyalty to a Person whose life has a magnetism to it. Following him is joy and fulfillment as well as a logically and empirically sound moral approach to life.

One day a friend and I were driving up the hill to our house when, in our quiet neighborhood, we saw a heated argument between a neighbor and his brother-in-law. They were not churchgoers, and I had tried to get them to consider a new direction for their lives. As we approached them, one opened a straight, barber's razor and slashed the other across his face, his ear, and a part of his neck. Blood pumped from his face as he fell, and his eyes were set. It took no thought, no delay, no comment—we dashed from my little Studebaker Champion, lifted him, applied a car seat pillow to cover the open gash in his face, and raced to the hospital.

We were in our late twenties. These men were ten years older, and huge. We were not social friends, and they were committed to another lifestyle entirely. None of that mattered. Here was a life carelessly being wasted, and in the name and spirit of Christ conscience had sounded the alarm; the bell had rung within. The physicians were shocked that he lived with so little blood left.

After that, we had the task of cleaning pints of blood from my car. And the person we saved never thanked us and still never showed up at our little church. But our action took no measure of any of that. It was only one example that could be copied countless times every day. When persons have the mind of Christ, when in loving obedience they have equipped their conscience with images of his words and his life, and when they are constrained by his cross and his living presence, they act as he would act.

WHEN CONSCIENCE NEEDS
REVIEWING

Because our values, loyalties, and priorities are learned and not inherited through our genes, and because they are buttressed and affirmed by habit and emotional attachment, they will not remain static, unchanged, and indelible. Because they comprise our conscience, the conscience itself will not remain static. Some behavior that shocked us twenty years ago will hardly raise an eyebrow now; and some conditions that we tolerated a generation ago we find revolting now. Homeless people have always been around, but our sensitivity toward them has been quickened, and today we find it repulsive that so many persons have nowhere to live.

It is the downside of this that needs so much attention—how

the demands of life, the incessant compromises, the constant negotiated settlements, the wearing down of idealism by the pressures to make money, to have money, and to conserve money seem somehow to numb the conscience. The moral thermometer works well, telling us *how we are* doing; but the thermostat is broken, failing to tell us *how we should be doing*.

I discovered very quickly that the simple, uncomplicated idealism that I acquired in seminary was always challenged by the situation at hand. I will never forget how a public relations firm helped us with a building fund campaign by giving us a list of potential donors who were known to have paid over $10,000 in income taxes per year. Where the list came from I never knew. Should we have accepted it? We never asked. Did it work? We raised $36,000 from the list. Was it right? In seminary I would have said no. But as I faced the financial burden of renovating a deteriorated church edifice, my conscience was numb on that issue concerning where the list came from.

Conscience can be toyed with for a long time before we find out that the alarm does not sound off any more. However, conscience can be renewed, revived, and restored. This can happen by allowing ourselves in sincere devotion to become more conscious of God's presence, God's love, God's mercy, and God's power. Religion is the source of moral earnestness, and a deeper trust in God has a cleansing effect. Isaiah, while having his vision in the temple, cried out, "I am a man of unclean lips. . . ."

Conscience can be repaired also by the simple acquisition of new facts. Once smoking cigarettes was regarded as a dirty habit that tainted one's breath and burned holes in overcoats, a habit that young boys picked up to look like Humphrey Bogart, Clark Gable, or Billy Ekstine. I practiced hard to learn how to inhale the smoke from cigarettes without choking. Then I found out later that smoking had actually killed the fathers of some of my best friends, whom we had thought died of "galloping consumption." Practically every adult male smoked something! So I quit. Conscience became informed, reprogrammed, and put on a new alert: no smoking!

New experiences can lift the conscience to new heights of sensitivity. Throughout my youth I had a friend who was blind, an orphan who was raised in foster homes and was a regular attendant of our Sunday school. Eventually, he became a preacher scholar with a Columbia Ph.D. He never wore shaded glasses, and his eyes drew much attention because they had never developed. They were a slate-colored mass of tissue with no hint of pupil, cornea, or iris. People stared at his eyes. One day as we talked about personal matters—preacher-to-preacher talk—I said, "Have you ever thought of wearing dark, shaded eyeglasses so that people will focus on your message and not focus on your blindness? You have too much of value to say, but I think that your eyes get all the attention." He asked me to go further. I continued, "You see, your eyes are a total gray mass, and eyes are normally one color or another at the center and surrounded by a white surface. But if you wore dark shades, no one would know what your eyes looked like and would focus on your presentation."

I will never forget his response: "Sam, you're talking like a person who knows colors, one who has seen gray, white, brown, green, and blue. If I could see colors, I would know what you're talking about, but I have never seen night or day, light or darkness. I live in a void with only a perception of size, sound, and distance, but I know nothing about color."

My soul! Conscience made another bounding leap, several notches higher. Since that day my new awareness of the isolation of total blindness has been a part of the equipment of my conscience. What we all need now is such an understanding of illiteracy, poverty, mental illness, sexual abuse, and racial discrimination in order that a new conscience on these matters would sound a national alarm.

Perhaps the greatest alteration in conscience came with marriage, when life had to turn from its inward concentration to an outward one, from an "I" concentration to a "we." Learning how to turn my mind away from my own private satisfactions and gratifications to a consideration of the gratifications and satisfactions of another called for a revision of my conscience. After marriage, every move I made was no longer an "I" action, but a "we."

Marriage can never be looked upon as a contractual, fifty-fifty relationship. Rather, each partner seeks to contribute to the good in the life of the other. As they continue to define that good that they seek mutually, each life is enriched. This, of course, is the ideal. (Unfortunately, many have no conception of such a joint pursuit, and two lives are locked in mutual destruction.) Marriage is the next step toward fulfillment of the total person after the basic processes of growth are accomplished.

Conscience is renewed also by exposure to other cultures. One day, in 1953, my mail brought an invitation to join two Baptist executives in visiting foreign missions in Europe, Palestine, India, and Burma—going to hospitals, colleges, Bible schools, secondary schools, and churches. I accepted and spent three months among persons whose diet, customs, religion, language, and opportunities were far different from my own.

The bottom line was that I saw how many dark-skinned people lived in the world and that they all had been colonized by Europeans. This gave me an authentic identity with Third-World people and their struggles for clean water, nutritious food, health care, safe housing, basic education, and hope for a brighter future.

Next, I saw how cheap life could be: humans scrounging for food all day every day; women with empty, dry breasts, reaching for a coin with fingers as thin as pencils; babies everywhere—on women's backs, in their arms, in their bodies, and held by the hand. Women were breeding machines.

I saw also how negative and ineffective Buddhism and Hinduism were in addressing the needs of Asians and Africans, how they taught the rejection of this world and focused on escape from this reality. I saw also why communism could find a home among persons with such beliefs about life and why Protestant communities with an accent on personal liberty, an open Bible, and the dignity of all persons would resist communism.

One night I "had it out" with "leftist" students in Jamshedpur, India. They scolded me for being an American and a black person. They thought I should have fled my country or shot myself. I explained that despite the injustices, I had accepted America as the place most likely to mature into a free, pluralistic society with individual liberties, a government by the consent of the governed, and an economy that could provide equal employment opportunities, housing, and education. I saw no other place in the world so well equipped ideologically and so well endowed socially and economically to achieve such goals. I thought they were going to kill me.

Moreover, that trip exposed me to cultural differences as well as how people of all cultures want basically the same things out of life: good health, economic well-being, education, leisure, security, and emotional and aesthetic satisfactions. And it exposed to me how privileged we were in America and how far short most of the people of the world fall from achieving those ends for their lives.

Conscience would never be the same. My alarms began to sound off in strange and different ways after my experience in Syria, Lebanon, Jordan, Israel, Turkey, Pakistan, India, Burma, and Western Europe.

Finally, conscience underwent a real metamorphosis when I became fully aware that social change in America was altogether too slow and the civil rights movement was an idea whose time had come. Both the oppressed and the oppressors had become habituated to a long-entrenched evil system of racist customs and behavior.

In the mid-1950s there emerged a son of a Georgia Baptist parsonage; a Morehouse, Crozer, and Boston University alumnus who seemed to have been a child of destiny: at the right place—Montgomery, Alabama; at the right time—when

George Wallace was governor; and the right person—a well-equipped, courageous, and committed young pastor. The story is well known. While he was serving as the Ph.D. pastor of a black, middle-class church—whose officers were college faculty members from nearby Alabama State College—a highly regarded black citizen named Rosa Parks refused to follow the rules and move to a segregated seat on the bus at the driver's command. She was arrested, and the conservative, well-adjusted, placid black community was sparked and fired by the deliberate, unrehearsed, unrelenting leadership of Martin Luther King, Jr., into a bus boycott.

King brought to that event the personal security of his rearing in a strong family; his Morehouse, Crozer, and Boston University education; and a quality of courage and commitment that is requisite for such a monumental contribution.

His church had a membership of persons with much higher than average education, and he did not want to have any traditional Baptist revivals. He preferred a "Spring Lecture Series." And I was fortunate enough to be invited to give those lectures. That meant spending a week with King at the very beginning of the boycott.

One night, as we slept in his modest parsonage, a deacon on guard dropped his baseball bat on the porch. He was napping, I suppose. I got up and went to the door to see if any harm had come. On my return to my bedroom I saw a light under King's bedroom door and knocked to see if he was all right. I found him reading, at 3 A.M., with a lamp on the floor, hanging halfway out of his bed. What was he reading? Paul Tillich's *Courage to Be*—at 3 A.M.!

His nagging problem was keeping enough gasoline on hand to fuel the volunteers' cars. The domestics and laborers who used buses had to get to work, and with a bus boycott a volunteer motor pool transported them. But the filling stations were threatened to deny them gasoline. So there was a need to explore out-of-town sources.

While I was there, King and I drove over to Tuskegee, a black town, to look for gas. A young Alabama state policeman tailed us, about two yards from the bumper of King's used Pontiac station wagon, from the Montgomery city limit to the Tuskegee city limit. We both perspired freely all the way. When we returned, the whole exercise was repeated.

All of this washed over my conscience, awakening me to a more poignant realization of the persistent evil intrinsic in a segregated society, the total negation of the humanity of those being excluded, and the limited means available to alter such a system. The tired and tedious method of the "pink tea and cookie" discussions had allowed evil to become more deeply entrenched and more difficult to remove.

Incidentally, in the fall of 1987 I was in Mobile for a conference, and a wild Gulf coast storm was approaching fast, with high winds and a floodtide. All hands scampered for an early departure. Flying was out; so I rented a Hertz Ford and raced through heavy rains to Montgomery and on to Atlanta. At Tuskegee I traveled the same road, wider and faster, that King and I had traveled with that trooper trailing us like a Gestapo agent. The road had been renamed Martin Luther King, Jr., Boulevard.

5

BELIEVING
in a World of Purpose

Normally we awaken each day and get started, carrying into our daytime activities a conscience that serves us fairly well and a settled set of assumptions about God, good and evil, and the nature of our human sojourn. Some of us begin the day with prayer, either at the bedside or at the breakfast table. Many families are better organized and take more time for Bible reading, reflection, and prayer. However we go about it, we carry with us into the day a "faith package," whether it is adequate or not. Others have tried to ignore this, but in actuality if they have no avowed faith of their own, they are likely to be cruising on the faith of their mothers or grandmothers—and without acknowledgment.

It is essential that we never try to deal with life and its choices without a well-nurtured faith. This is what keeps conscience alert and responsive, the reaffirmation of *whose* we are and *in whom* we believe. As I approached that plateau of life where parenting and careerism become so demanding, I found the strength and support that I needed in the religious faith that I had kept alive. Obviously there were some changes in my world view, in my understanding of who the devil was, where heaven and hell were located, and what happened after death; yet I had held onto answers to all these issues that keep my inner life coherent.

THE VORTEX OF CHANGE

When I was a student at Virginia Union University, I never dreamed that my wife, Bessie, and I would return there one day with me as a professor and with two sons. However, after my three years at Crozer Seminary and a year at Yale Graduate School, I persevered, survived the interruption caused by our first son's heart illness, and completed the doctor of theology degree at Boston University. I had begun a serious intellectual adventure in religion and philosophy at Virginia Union while in college, and it lasted throughout. Big questions troubled me, and I demanded working answers. So I found teaching exciting from 1949 to 1955, but in the spring of 1955 our esteemed and devoted university president, John McEllison, announced his retirement; and at age thirty-three I was chosen to lead my dear alma mater. What a frightening thing to happen so early in my life, and I went at it with yeoman's earnestness! The problems were staggering, and I worked incessantly.

The kind of moral education that I had brought from home and the Bank Street Baptist Church made me feel that work was the means by which I expressed gratitude for blessings unmerited. Also, I liked financial sufficiency and independence. So in college I had worked in the dining hall at every job; in seminary I worked in the kitchen, in the president's home, on the grounds, in the post office, at Sears and Roebuck, and at washing and greasing Bond Bread trucks. In the end I managed the bookstore. All of this came easily because of the satisfaction of being independent.

The unlimited scope of the work of the college president drafted me into the center of the arena of public trust, and I felt it. At that early age I felt looked up to; and the investment of the trust that students, parents, faculty, alumni, trustees, community leaders, and church people placed in me was burdensome. Moreover, the world was in a maelstrom of change, and I felt as if I were on the edge of its vortex. Many problems were immediate: keeping students contented, maintaining faculty morale, meeting the payrolls and guarding the cash flow, protecting our accreditation, and recruiting good students. My plate was full. Yet I could not escape involvement in the flood of change rising all around me. I was on a platform perpetually, giving speeches and sermons constantly. I was busily drafting something to say whenever I sat down in quietness.

This challenge pointed directly to my belief system, my faith hypotheses, the anchor for my soul. Did I believe sufficiently to support such draining and wearing and buffeting? Was my scaffolding of faith sufficient to carry the load? Did my life have at its center an integrative, whole-making core of assumptions that did not need to be tested every day but remained intact? When questions were hurled at me from students, from the press, and in conversations with local leaders, did my answers reflect a reliable, resolute belief system that rang with assurance?

THE END OF AN ERA

None of us knew exactly how to behave when segregation ended. We had had so much rehearsal at living in a separate world that we knew the protocol of segregated dining. Whenever we had been driving from Virginia to New York City, for example, we all knew to go to the bathroom in Washington, D.C. We could not be sure of any clean and usable rest rooms being available to blacks traveling two and a half hours up U.S. Route 1 to Baltimore, and Maryland's Route 40 to the old Esso station where U.S. Route 13 joined Route 40, entering Delaware. Then, we had to make it somehow to New Brunswick, New Jersey, from the Chester-Bridgeport ferry because for the entire length of New Jersey Route 130, through south Jersey, we dared not stop. That was life.

Well, while I was a college president in Virginia, the NAACP sued for school integration, and I was all over the South speaking several times a week advocating this change. My stock speech was "The Power of an Idea Whose Time Has Come." When the 1954 Supreme Court decision came down, along with the subsequent decision of 1955, we knew that the end of an era had come. The questions were, Would all whites move to outlying districts to avoid integrated schools? Would whites accept blacks as teachers? Will private schools rise up everywhere for whites, leaving underfinanced public schools for blacks? Would there be riots? Will buses be burned?

I was thrust into the center of all of these issues, both on the platforms and in closed-door sessions. Now and then a white group would involve me in real, honest dialogue, and occasionally a major platform before whites would be open to me. The Jewish Women's Club of Richmond—an educated group of stylish young mothers, many from Northern origins—defied custom and had me address their weekly lecture series at the old Byrd Hotel in Richmond, Virginia. At the end of the 1955 lecture series, the lunch meetings of their club moved to the YWCA. I did not know why. All I knew was that the following year we met at the "Y" and not at the hotel. That was in 1955 and 1956. Well, in *1986* I was asked to come down from New Jersey for a lecture, thirty years later. The club members had all looked good in 1956; but in 1986 they looked much better, ripened with age, grandmothers with soft creases in their faces, their foreheads marked with the etchings of decades of loving with the selfless love of mothers. They were seasoned, quick-witted, verbal, gentle, and looking satisfied with life. I had remembered them well. But the point is that they finally told me that the hotel had ordered them to cancel my appearances there in 1956 or move! They moved, but did not tell me why for thirty years!

Every time I appeared before a black audience, I was deeply aware of the total range of their life experiences: from bitter insults to private moments of joy, from fear of the next day's developments to a resilient faith in the One who holds the future. I could not go before them shaky, ambiguous, or undecided. They looked to me to give them something to hold on to. Meanwhile, I saw myself as a bridge between the races and a bridge between two eras. It required spiritual strength and poise to be that kind of bridge with integrity.

Let me share two provocative occurrences. The moment

came in Richmond, for example, to have an integrated dinner for the Red Feather–Community Chest Campaign at the fabulous John Marshall Hotel for the first time. I was chairman of "Unit 7," the campaign for the "colored" contributions. (Even these funds were raised on a racially separate basis.) I sat at the table with a most saintly and benevolent white pastor of the largest church in town. As we chatted, a large, dark-skinned hand reached down between us to place a soup bowl on the table, and my eyes traced up the sleeve to see whose hand it was; it belonged to a wonderfully fine father of two of our students at the college. He was "moonlighting" as a waiter. He smiled at me with pride that at last he had "made it" to the John Marshall.

When he was coming back with another dish, my friend, the pastor was commenting very negatively about a certain outstanding black leader. And as my black waiter friend approached, I bumped my white pastor friend with my knee to stop his comments. I feared that my black waiter friend would hear what he was saying, which would do no one any good at all. He said, "Did you bump me?" "Yes," I replied. "I didn't want the waiter to hear your comments on a man he knew well." He said, "The waiter? I haven't seen a waiter; did you?"

He saw the hand reach between us, but it was like a stick or a rope—not a human form. It belonged to no one—yet it *did*. (The two sons of that man are now both lawyers, one a state senator and the other a municipal judge, in that same Richmond.) My balancing act could get delicate, but I saw my "bridge" role as crucial. We had a future to face, and our chances for succeeding could be improved with more "bridge" persons.

I preached in the Duke University chapel one warm spring Sunday morning. Chaplain Wilkerson told me that a former president had said that a "colored" preacher would preach there over his dead body. When I asked where he was buried, Wilkinson pointed to a crypt under the pulpit where I was sitting! One ought to be careful with such threats.

As I left Duke, driving toward Richmond, two white fellows

had inscribed in lipstick on the back of a poster "Ashland, Va."
I was going almost to Ashland and wondered if they would
accept a ride with me. My collar was open, tie on the seat, and
I had on sunshades. Would they accept? I pulled over. They
conferred rather long. I waited, and they came. I asked where
they had been. They answered they had been to chapel at Duke
with their girlfriends, whom they were visiting. They were
from Randolph-Macon College. I asked about the sermon, and
they said that it was the first time they had heard a black
speaker and that more whites should have such a chance because it would make integration much easier. Then one noticed my picture on the poster they had used, and he shouted,
"Hey! Bubba, it's him; he's the one." We launched into a most
penetrating conversation.

The school integration crisis was followed by the Montgomery bus boycott with Dr. Martin Luther King, Jr. As I said, an
era was ending, and some of us were determined to see that
the transition succeeded. This conviction was not something
forced upon me but, rather, was the reflection of my beliefs.
Throughout all my activities and involvement in the rapid
changes that transpired in America from 1955 to 1969, I operated out of beliefs that comprised my central pivot of religious
faith.

THIS IS THE
BEST WORLD POSSIBLE

At the very beginning of my belief system stands the faith
proposition that this world, planet earth, is the best one God
could make for the purposes that God sought to accomplish.
In other words, I start out accepting the world as *good,* and
whatever problems with it that I may have result from my
own lack of knowledge or understanding. I cannot make it
through the day believing that God actually had a better world
in mind but kept it from us. Also, I am a monotheist. There
are no other gods out there; there is no one like a "red devil"
running loose. The term "devil" is used to account for the

absence of the good, but I never allowed that God had a "competitor" somewhere in the world.

Of course, this opens up the whole problem of a Bible written by inspired writers of the ancient world being taken literally throughout, taking the writings out of their historical context. The Bible is a record of the experiences of a believing people, but God gave us Christ in the "fulness of time." We cannot deny the Christian view of God that we were given in Christ in order to hold onto an ancient view that reflected a more primitive understanding of the nature of God. Christians must read the Bible with the lenses of Christian truths. After all, before one line of the Old Testament was written, God *was*—full, complete, and in charge. The Old Testament did not create God. Rather, it is a record of the experiences of a nomadic people in a prescientific age without compass, telescope, ruler, calendar, typewriter, or camera. Everything was passed on by word of mouth, relying on the accuracy of one another's memory. There was no printing press. Each book was copied by hand on sheepskin or papyrus, subject also to the religious views of the one doing the copying. So it is our task to heed their witness and then seek the Lord for ourselves in the light of our current knowledge—after telescopes, microscopes, astronomy, archaeology, and the study of the whole ancient world have all instructed our search for the living God.

Following the teachings of Christ, I accept the world as *good*. Our finite knowledge has not yet fathomed all its secrets. We have unlocked the mysteries of tuberculosis, yellow fever, and heart transplants, but diabetes, AIDS, and many mental illnesses still defy us. God has given us the genius, the brain cells, to pursue the perfection of creation. Our time on this stage is brief, but among the items on our agenda while here are the cultivation of the mind as an end itself, i.e., a part of our *becoming,* and a world with enough mystery in it to tease us into exploration and discovery that it is a good world.

While we are here for our brief tour, another achievement for us is to see how far we can advance from basic animal survival behavior toward the paragon of selfless love that we find in Jesus. Before our son's miraculous heart surgery at Johns Hopkins in 1960, his illness was the center of our lives. It seemed that the little hole in his infant heart was allowed to be there to slow us all down in our hot pursuit of private goals and to get some practice at altruism. Rev. Thomas B. Davis and his lovely, wife, Antoinette, friends in Baltimore, opened their home to us for thirty-nine overnight visits from Richmond. Today, my antennae resonate to suffering in the lives of others in ways they never could without the training my heart received in sharing the isolation and the risks of our little boy. Through the Christian Children's Fund we pay for the monthly support of a Moslem boy attending a Catholic secondary school in a French-speaking West African country. This endeavor comes about so easily because of the rehearsal we had in responding to our son's need.

God knows what we need. When Johns Hopkins told us to find forty-eight pints of blood and that none could be bought in Baltimore, we were floored. Where on earth would we get it? Friends in Richmond could not give through the Red Cross. At that time, the Red Cross did not take "colored" blood, even though a "colored" hematologist, Dr. Charles Drew, developed the blood bank that saved millions of "colored" and white soldiers in World War II.

I was preaching one Sunday morning in Petersburg, twenty-five miles away, and my host asked me about my son. I told him about the need for the blood. He told someone else, and as word spread, the football coach of our arch-rival team in Petersburg heard of it. The next thing we knew was that the tiny hole in the ventricular septum of our son's heart had caused forty-eight football players to stop practice early, go to a Red Cross trailer parked in rural Virginia in order to circumvent the "no colored blood" rule in Richmond, and donate blood for our son's surgery. These ball players were introduced to the whole concept of the saving power of blood, the goodness of giving of oneself, and the idea of taking on another's need and suffering by virtue of that tiny leak in the ventricular septum. God knows the kind of world we need.

The desperate hunger that kills millions of children each year in Ethiopia, Somalia, and other nations on the edge of the Sahara will cause us to learn charity with the same diligence that we now learn computer science and will make feeding the hungry look as practical as making money. We will harness and redirect our proneness to cling to every known advantage with the same agility and success that we now harness the atom and create nuclear energy. And, paradoxically, we can no more afford to have 4 billion people cleaning teeth with sticks and one billion with toothbrushes than we can afford to use the nuclear weapons we have perfected. The lion and the lamb, indeed, shall lie down together. God's world will teach us that and more.

FREEDOM TO CHOOSE OUR
OWN CONSTRAINTS

The next principle in my belief system is that the same God who made the world out of nothing, and left in it enough mystery and challenge to compel us to excel as the crowning of all creation, gave us real freedom and the power of choice. Indeed, we are conditioned by genes, culture, parenting, and political and economic restraints, but a margin of choice remains. We are not predetermined. Though nature and environment have done all that they can do to shape and mold us, the final outcome is ours to determine.

One of the great opportunities of a college president is to observe outcomes from modest beginnings in his or her students. At North Carolina A&T State University, where I began as president in 1960, the Reverend Jesse Jackson was our quarterback and the president of our student body. And with all of his ability and drive, even then I could never have imagined that he would have used his freedom to such an amazing degree. I would look a lot younger had I not had Jesse as the student body president!

Likewise, sitting in a position of influence and prestige exposes one to many other uses of freedom. During the early

sixties I went to give an address at a convocation at Wake
Forest University. It was on the theme of racial justice, and
most students and faculty were sympathetic. I had a big round
of applause when introduced. But not everyone felt good
about this. As I spoke, a male student in the curtain wings
behind me screamed and ran across the stage completely
naked. A "streaker," they called him. I simply said, "Are there
any other volunteers before I go on?" Whenever such a response came forth, it tightened my jaws, stiffened my spine,
and put more authority in my voice. Some used their freedom
in childish, resentful ways, as instruments of reaction.

Contrariwise, others came forth with unpretentious charity
and understanding. In 1964, I was asked to give the commencement address at Lenoir Rhyne College in the Piedmont
section of North Carolina. In the sixties that took presidential
gall! I was grateful for the opportunity and gave my stock
"integration speech" to an all-white audience of parents,
grandparents, cousins, aunts, and uncles—primarily plain
folk from rural North Carolina. When I finished, I was approached by an elderly couple standing close together, smiling at me with joyous approval and extending their hands;
their jeweled eyes twinkled like stars. There was human goodness written on their faces while the wrinkles of age receded
behind a smile of sweet release. I will never forget them,
gray-haired, bent, and reaching out to me.

They handed me a small box, neatly wrapped and tied with
a white, silk ribbon. They said that their grandson was gradu-
ating, but the gift they had brought for him they wanted me
to have, for they would buy him another. I still have it: a Cross
pen and pencil set. I also have a watch that the A&T students
gave me that same year, presented by Jesse Jackson. One was
a symbol of understanding and acceptance, a token of reconciling love. The other was a symbol of student unrest and the
drive for change. My soul! What a way to use the freedom that
God has given us, to work for and to accept change, amelioration, and reconcilation!

I had a visit from a high political appointee while I was

associate Peace Corps director. He was an officer in a very large church and a leader in a major metropolitan center of America. His brilliant and affable pastor was in trouble, having assembled a harem of beautiful women, all wives of outstanding leaders in the church and the community. Now this pastor was well educated, experienced, and familiar with human foibles in history, literature, and among his friends and parishioners. He was no novice, but here is how he had used his freedom: he had attended a training institute that prepared counselors to help persons to come out of their tight, narrow, and destructive egocentricity and to be relaxed, giving, and secure. It was a "touchy and feely" group experience, with all the potential of becoming another sexual explosion. And it did. The "touchy-feely" aspect got ahead of the larger purposes, and he ended up going to bed with a dozen of the leading lights.

Here came the problem: this highly placed church officer wanted us to lift his pastor out of that mess and waft him away to some exotic, tropical, "Third World" country, where he could gain some anonymity and make a fresh start. Fine, except that the Peace Corps was recruiting answers, not problems. We were not an asylum for undisciplined, hedonistic, pathological, displaced pastors. With deepest sympathy we had to acknowledge that the pastor had terribly misused his freedom, of which the consequences were discreetly spread all over that town.

During the days of change, 1955–1969—days of the Vietnam protests; the civil rights marches; the decolonization of Asia, Africa, and the islands of the seas; the riots in cities and on campuses; the social legislation and iconoclastic Supreme Court decisions—many persons had great difficulty adjusting to change. They saw the merit in the changes sought, but their freedom was fettered. They were bound to old customs and folkways. Wrong had been tolerated so long that it had become habit.

In my sermons I struggled hard to translate the experiences of the apostle Paul into current thought. Paul's background was Judaism and its legalism. He spoke of how the proscriptions of that legalism crushed him with guilt and condemnation. He could not keep track of his violations. The law did not create goodness; it assigned guilt. He said that his members "warred" within him, and he was always wanting to do what he should not and actually doing what he would not. But when he surrendered his will to Christ, believed that Christ was the gracious gift of God, that his life was God's token of love to lift us Godward, this faith transformed him and made him the captive of the mind of Christ. He said *he* no longer lived but *Christ* lived in him. In practical terms, he lived so that the true spirit of the law was truly fulfilled in him, but it was by the grace of God empowering him from within. Paul called it the victory in Christ.

I found great joy in preaching this central, core Christian message and not getting detoured by debating those parts of the Bible that reflected sub-Christian moral standards. I saw them as the historical reflection of what the experience was like in trying to grasp the true spirit of God. In Acts 17:30 there is the phrase: "And the times of this ignorance God winked at. . . ." Every Bible student should ponder that, for it is a candid observation that there were some perceptions of God's will that were incomplete in earlier times.

Much of our problem with religious faith is in where we begin: the world is filled with mystery, earthquakes, genetic flaws, unexplained diseases, evil happening to good people, and undeserving people living well. Yet much of this we can deal with if we first believe that God provided us the best world possible, given all that God wanted us to become, and that much of the remaining mystery—wars, hunger, racism, genocide, gender discrimination, and the like—is attributable to the freedom that we have. This is a freedom to be passive, lazy, uncommitted, and numb to life, as well as the freedom to be self-directing, involved, charitable, empathetic, altruistic, and alive to the times.

Most of all, it is the freedom to take all of life's gifts and place them under the constraint of a spiritual ideal, and for

Christians that ideal is the constraint of Christ, so that we say with Paul, "I live; yet not I, but Christ liveth in me" (Galatians 2:20).

JESUS: HUMAN AND DIVINE

I have learned to show great patience with those who take a longer time to accept Jesus as the Son of God. Likewise, I have great suspicion of those who clap their hands, close their eyes, and accept this faith proposition without thought. To me it is the most consequential decision that one can make, for in it one is saying that the God who created the vast universe, with distances between solar systems that the human mind cannot measure and with a spaciousness that trails on into an infinite "never," chose planet earth to be designed for human life, equipped for being with thought, reflection, language, curiosity, analysis, and enduring faith. And on planet earth this God set forth a person of matchless love, of unmixed charitable impulses, of transparent moral intention, and of a selfless, sacrificial spirit. His name is Jesus. He was born into a humble Jewish family, an heir to the long history of the Jewish people, beginning with Abraham looking for a city with foundations; proceeding with Moses and the deliverance from Egypt; ascending with Elijah to Mount Carmel in the name of the one true God; and amplified, refined, and epitomized in the resounding proclamations of the prophets Micah, Amos, and Isaiah.

He spent his youth in Nazareth, as a carpenter's son, with sisters and brothers, learning about the habits of ants, fig trees, snakes, and fish, and studying the birds that were fed by the finger of God and the lilies of the field in their casual and unassuming beauty. At about age twelve, when all young people start putting it all together, he became conscious of the rumors about his miraculous birth and heard the stories about Simeon and Anna, the wise men, and the barn in Bethlehem; and there rose in his consciousness those immortal words of the prophet of old: "The Spirit of the Lord GOD is upon me;

because the LORD hath anointed me to preach good tidings unto the meek; he hath sent me to bind up the brokenhearted, to proclaim liberty to the captives, and the opening of the prison to them that are bound" (Isaiah 61:1).

The events of his life from then on indicated that God had chosen this life through whom there would be revealed the paragon of human possibilities, and in this life would be poured all the divine attributes that a human life could embrace. Moreover, all of us would be magnetized toward this goodness by the power of the love and grace found in him.

> Thou seemest human and divine,
> The highest holiest manhood thou;
> Our wills are ours we know not how,
> Our wills are ours to make them thine.

Indeed, in the first century of the Christian era many set their hands to write about this life, as Luke states in the opening of his biography of Jesus. Much of what was written about him the church rejected as unfounded, exaggerated, plainly false, or too thin to be preserved as the truth. Doubtless, some material that *was* included in the four Gospels and that did make the canon "leaked" into the record from that body of bizarre and unaccredited stories that had been in circulation. We will never know for certain, but, thank God, we have enough to give us the portrait of the life we honor as the Son of God. And it matches the portrait of the one Isaiah had seen with his prophetic vision six hundred years before:

For he shall grow up before him as a tender plant, and as a root out of a dry ground: he hath no form nor comeliness; and when we shall see him, there is no beauty that we should desire him. He is despised and rejected of men; a man of sorrows, and acquainted with grief: and we hid as it were our faces from him; he was despised, and we esteemed him not. Surely he hath borne our griefs, and carried our sorrows: yet we did esteem him stricken, smitten of God, and afflicted. But he was wounded for our transgressions, he was bruised for our iniquities: the chastisement of our peace was upon him; and with his stripes we are healed (Isaiah 53:2–5).

105

Among the beliefs in my faith structure is the conviction that Jesus is uniquely given to us as the Bright and Morning Star, the Lily of the Valley, and the Rose of Sharon, the anointed One. This is not only because of the record but because of the self-authenticating nature of his teachings and his example. When we put to the test—to any test whatever—what he taught and how he lived it turns out that it is the only way for us to proceed in our personal lives or as a people, a society, or a nation without chaos and self-destruction. The positive, agressive effort to find our own worth by seeking worth in others is axiomatic. The reverse of such effort is destructive. To grant others the privileges and priorities and prerogatives that we demand for ourselves is the painful truth toward which the world is slowly staggering. To gain one's life by losing it in something better is the answer to drug use, divorce, suicide, and poor grades in school. Indeed, Jesus is the way, the truth, and the life. And to believe in something so abstract and amorphous as the eternal love of God for lepers, children who are epileptic, beggars, habitual sinners, and thieves to the extent that one would suffer death on a cross, transcends all of the cheap and convenient compromises by which we live and causes him to hold such a victory over this mortal corruption that he leads us all in triumph over death and the grave, marching off the edge of time into eternal life.

I believe that those who believe in this unique divinity of Christ and whose loyalty to his life and teaching as central are brought thereby closer to God and within the orbit of God's healing power. It is the answer to tension, fitful insecure living, obsessive self-aggrandizement, and indolent, unproductive living. The fact is that such belief does confer "power to become."

THE IMMANENT POSSIBILITY
OF THE KINGDOM OF GOD

Jesus devoted much of his brief three-year ministry speaking of the kingdom of God. We today are not moved by the image of kings, royalty, and blind obeisance paid to any human; so when God is pictured as a king, something is lost in the translation to our time. Nevertheless, there were kings in Christ's day and there had been kings for thousands of years. Everyone knew of the absolute authority of a king. So when Jesus spoke of the kingdom of God, it was clear what he meant.

He called us to serve as subjects of a King who had no throne, who had no army, no brass-braided generals and deputies, and no palace with servants at his feet. This kingdom was invisible, voluntarily joined, and bound together by the decision of each member, one at a time, to obey the teachings of God as presented by Jesus Christ. This kingdom did not solicit group memberships, nations, states, or races as members. It required a personal, one-at-a-time commitment; and if an entire group, race, or nation made such a commitment, so might it be.

Members of God's kingdom were peacemakers; they loved with the kind of love that sought good in the lives of others; to them a neighbor was anyone who was hungry, thirsty, or victimized by poverty or exclusion; they forgave seventy times seven; their main purpose was to seek and to save the lost; they found their own lives by losing them for the sake of Christ; their lives were flavored with the aroma of the gospel of Christ.

During a period of change and challenge, 1955–1962, I realized that an important corollary to my faith in Jesus Christ as our spiritual leader and Lord was that this kingdom of God that he proclaimed was a real possibility. There is always the temptation to dream of a social and political utopia in which there is no pain and suffering and everyone lives a fulfilled life. This is an outcome worth dreaming about, but the idea of the kingdom of God reaches us right where we are and calls us all to accept the rulership, the regnancy of the will of God in our lives now and where we are. And that will of God is what we find manifested in Jesus Christ. So with Jesus as the center of our moral and spiritual consciousness, it follows that such a consciousness leads us into God's rulership over our lives. One's behavior is governed by the mind of Christ.

During these turbulent years my belief in a world of purpose enabled me to understand and appreciate the changes that were being pursued. Some persons, no doubt, are motivated to work for change out of a purely secular orientation, with a goal of providing an improved quality of life for everyone, with no reference to God at all. When one is impelled by the rulership of God, however, the changes sought are in obedience to God's will. One is moved to show God's love and regard for every life, as a creation of God; to bring about those circumstances in which every child of God can enjoy the abundant life; and to serve the needs of the hurting people everywhere in fulfillment of our loyalty to the teachings and example of Christ.

There are differences according to our motivation to work for change, and the first difference lies in the strategies and tactics available to us. The struggle for change led by the NAACP culminated in thirty-nine Supreme Court victories, the 1954 school integration case being the last of them. One of the first was the teacher salary equalization case of 1935. I went to school one day and found that our resplendent, dignified, stylish biology teacher, Alene Black, was absent. She was one of the main reasons for the boys going to school at all! But she had been fired for suing for equal pay based on equal qualification with the white teachers. So had been J. Ruppert Picott in Hampton and Lutrelle Palmer in Newport News, two truly courageous and sacrificing persons. Steven J. Wright in Maryland and others were fired for threatening to sue!

Furthermore, the strategy engaged by Martin L. King, Jr., and his associates was one of nonviolence, of active involvement but passive resistance to violence. In Christ the power of active, redemptive love is the weapon used against evil. It is not cowardice. The New Testament presents a Jesus of strength and courage, but not one of violence. King's method worked, and following his death the program that erupted in street violence interrupted the moral momentum that King had generated. We can all understand hot anger, the impetuousness, the indignation of young blacks who were weary of their futile existence. But if one should see their neighborhoods today, it is clear that their strategy was futile as well.

Obedience to God as a kingdom dweller often brings one into serious conflict with the pragmatic programs of practical politics. This is the second difference. The goals of the kingdom of God are infinitely more far-reaching than the immediate goals of a political agenda, a racial strategy, or a national program. All these may be benefited wonderfully as we follow Christ's leadership into the kingdom, but the Christian believes not only that God's purposes in the world as revealed in Christ are primary but that the interests of all people are best served in obedience to God's will in Jesus Christ.

Obviously, the stumbling block is that persons will confuse the kingdom of God with the physical church on the corner of Broad and Elm, acres of fine parked cars, an air-conditioned sanctuary, a million-dollar organ and an endowment. Indeed, possibly, the program of such a church and the claims of the kingdom may be in perfect harmony. But the general rule is that the moral commitment of such an institution is so fragile and so dependent on a consensus, with evil motives heavily influencing each decision, that we are more likely to find God's kingdom among certain members individually than in the church as an institution.

One of the disgraces of the era of change was the weak witness and the cowardly accommodation of so many churches to social reaction. The so-called "right wing" in America found its strongest ally among weak and uncommitted churches.

The kingdom of God is, therefore, not the church, although the two should be parallel. The kingdom of God is above and beyond institutional limitations, although it may include persons in any institutions. It is wherever the will of God as revealed in Jesus is being lived out. It is not co-terminal with any national boundary, for nations have purposes and agendas that fall short of the kingdom's ideals, and their very existence often is bound to racial and cultural homogeneity that does not imply moral and spiritual homogeneity.

The kingdom of God is more than an ethereal desire or wish; it presses toward practical expression. I found myself one day, for example, in the poor eastern, tobacco-growing, farm area of North Carolina giving a speech to a 4-H Club conference. The thirteen-year-old who introduced me had severely crossed eyes. It worried me, and I located his parents to see if I could start some movement toward getting his eyes straightened. At first, they rejected the whole idea as being against God's will. I debated with them and won, but how would I get this done?

I sat at my desk in Greensboro dreaming about it, and the idea came to ask Dr. Waldo Beach, a highly respected professor of Christian Ethics at the Duke University Divinity School, if he knew any ophthalmologists in the Durham medical fraternity who might straighten these eyes *gratis*. He did, and they did! It was a miracle. There I was thinking "kingdom thoughts," and I hooked up with a kingdom dweller—praise God! And he hooked up with kingdom-dwelling ophthalmologists. The ways of the kingdom prevailed in very practical, discreet, explicit ways: crossed eyes were straightened.

I recall how a telephone call from New York to my desk at Virginia Union University in Richmond summoned me to New York City to confer with the aide of one of the world's leading philanthropists. My assignment was to organize a survey across the South, in the wake of adamant resistance to school desegregation and threats of awesome violence, to find out what money—unlimited—could do to lessen tensions. Period. I teamed up with my friend and colleague, the late Thomas H. Henderson, and we managed to set up twenty conferences, four hours each, in extremely hospitable and clandestine living rooms across the South. We met in urban and university centers; with black and white leadership from business, religious, educational, and political circles; men and women; young and not so young. In six weeks of intensive travel we discovered that money would *exacerbate* tensions, not *lessen* them. Money would fuel the flames locally. No one could think of how local institutions could morally use money except to press harder for integration. Bribes were out, and tensions would last until desegregation was accomplished.

However, we did learn that all standard institutions that had been laboring for years in race relations were ineffective in many ways because of lack of funds. Many of these were interracial, but all were working at changing the social climate in favor of integration. This philanthropist accepted our recommendation to strengthen them, resulting in literally millions of dollars funding those anemic institutions and fostering their agendas. The kingdom is not restricted. It breaks out into form and substance in least expected ways.

Perhaps the most challenging aspect of the kingdom of God is its inclusiveness.

But He introduced a new inclusiveness. The kingdom of God is open to Syrophoenicians, Romans, Samaritans, Greeks, and "whosoever will"! Jesus looked beneath cultural and political loyalties and accretions and saw persons capable of responding to God's love, a new relationship that would alter *all other* relationships. That is exactly what I came to believe. I was free, therefore, to work for racial and economic justice and free, likewise, to love everybody!

Perhaps the most difficult problem is to reconcile the claims of the kingdom with political expediency and priorities. I recall President Dwight Eisenhower calling a group of black citizens to the White House in 1955 to confer with us about school integration and racial tensions. Here we sat with the president in the White House, listening to him tell approximately sixty black educators, clergymen, business leaders, and civil rights activists that we should "ease up" on our quest for integration. He failed. Every person in the room felt that the 1954 Supreme Court decision was the most redemptive act we had witnessed since Rutherford B. Hayes shut down the Reconstruction in 1876. It was a new legal plateau on which we planned to stand to launch other crusades for freedom. The decision acknowledged our basic humanity, rejected our

111

inferior status, contested our exclusion, and affirmed our dignity. For a president to ask us to defer our acceptance of it was an embarrassment and an insult. Eisenhower was a decent man, but he was a politician. And his political allegiances ran counter to the claims of God's kingdom.

One of the strangest and most enlightening experiences of this era was my trip to the Soviet Union. I had a nagging curiosity about life in Russia, which I was able to satisfy when the Baptist World Alliance asked me to join a team of three to go and preach in Russian Baptist churches. We stopped on the way to see Auschwitz, Warsaw, Prague, and East Berlin; while there, we also went into Riga in Latvia. I had already traveled in India, Burma, and the Near East, the lasting benefits of such I knew quite well.

So on the Russian trip I took note of everything. I suppose I was selected to demonstrate that America was aware of its need to change its worldwide image concerning its black citizens. On each visit I was free and uninstructed, and I told the whole truth about racial matters in the United States. It was painful at times to describe our history and the awful paradoxes that existed. But the fact was that everywhere I went there were no blacks at all, except entertainers and artists. Europe has no black presence, and the plight of blacks in England is scandalous.

One would have to be black to know what it is like to be an American with footnotes on one's citizenship, to have to explain the ambiguous nature of one's existence, and then to declare loyalty to one's country and a clear intention to remain there forever. My listeners never know quite what to make of our status, because economically our average income is better than that of most people in Europe; and, on the average, no other people in the world is better educated and in better health. Yet even with these "American" advantages, it is still an embarrassment to have to explain the negative attitudes toward us and the limits placed on our upward mobility.

After my graduate training and those four years in Providence, I had reached the point at which I could judge America, judge other societies, and judge the black struggle itself in the light of the claims of Christ and the ethic of the kingdom of God. After studying Christian ethics with Bainton, Pope, and Niebuhr at Yale and New Testament ethics with Booth at Boston University, my head was clear. I had no chauvinistic, absolute, national, or ethnic loyalties that inhibited me in judging my country or my race in the light of the transcendent, redemptive claims of kingdom loyalties.

When I visited Eastern Europe and the Soviet Union I was very much aware of being in a closed society. Our team could not travel freely. We were escorted at all times. In Prague we could not leave the hotel at night because we had no passports—because the authorities had collected them from us. We were advised against preaching certain sermons about Jesus in the Baptist churches. Once I aimed my camera at a rural home with neat stacks of wood piled in endless columns, and a hand reached out and covered my lens. I was accused of photographing a "poverty" scene. It was far from that.

The antireligious posture of the government and the students seemed compelled. In the churches there was such emotion, such tearful worship, such joyous singing, such long services with people standing inside for three hours and others waiting outside to get in. It was hard to believe that religious sentiment had been banished from universities and government. All this heightened my appreciation for a society governed by the governed; freedom of assembly; freedom to march, to petition, to protest; freedom to make jokes about the president; freedom to worship in whatever way one wishes; and freedom to read anything. It seemed to me that the kingdom of God could find manifestation in a free society with much greater access than in the closed ones I saw.

Speaking of the application of the kingdom to practical, live situations, there may be some gray areas in which the claims of the kingdom are not clear, but I judge that to be our fault in clouding those claims that call for some personal sacrifice. In the period 1955–1962, the movement for black liberation

113

and the removal of every trace of racism began to gather momentum. A new trend developed that went beyond working toward inclusion and equality. It was a movement toward separatism and rejection of white society and culture entirely. The black community was terribly divided because many had no quarrel with what America was all about. They *wanted in.* The new trend sought to establish stronger alliances with African nations, peoples, and cultures. A movement began to gain support that called for blacks to assert their identity, not with America, but with their African roots.

In this, there was a truly noble sentiment: to affirm black contributions, ancient and contemporary, and to learn more about black history and the struggle for sheer survival. With some effort schools responded, and today such an emphasis enjoys grudging support in most places. But in this trend was something else—an isolationism, a withdrawal, an angry resentment, and a consuming bitterness. Since it was unrealistic and impractical for blacks to walk off their jobs at General Motors, AT&T, the county hospital, the navy yard, the textile mill, the Department of the Treasury, the Hilton Hotel, CBS, the public schools, the post office, and the local bank, they were left in constant association with whites but with no working assumption on how to relate to them.

The kingdom of God fosters the fight for justice and equality without equivocation. Jesus went to the cross in pursuit of the abundant life for all persons, especially those farthest out. The kingdom was heralded by the majestic words of Isaiah, as young Jesus read them in the synagogue, beginning, "The Spirit of the Lord is upon me . . ." (Luke 4:18, quoting from Isaiah 61:1). This kingdom calls for reconciliation and aggressive love, for seeking opportunities for mutual reassessment of belligerent positions. Jesus is unequivocal on that. It was difficult for many of us to find a place in a movement that countenanced violence, bitterness, and intransigent ethnocentricity. We all knew the pain and suffering and what our options were. More hatred was not an option.

In this case, those of us who were in education and government programs had to find our way to create new openings for progress and change, as well as show support for other efforts as opportunities came. I recall that a phone call to the president's home awakened me close to midnight as the Freedom Riders' bus approached Greensboro. (This group was headed for Birmingham to challenge "Bull" Connor's reign of tight racial segregation. The ride was widely publicized, and everyone knew that violence would await the riders in Alabama and all along the way.) The call came from Simeon Booker, an old schoolmate and a fellow "sufferer" in Latin and Greek. We were the only two left! He had become the editor of *Jet* magazine, the weekly digest of black life in America. I remember Simeon saying to me as we surrendered ourselves for a Latin final back in 1941:

> Sam, Latin is a dead language.
> It died across the sea.
> It killed all the Romans,
> And now it's killing me!

Simeon informed me that the bus was approaching Greensboro and the people had no food and nowhere to sleep. He wanted to know if I, the president of a state-owned black college in North Carolina, would get up, find someone to prepare food and make arrangements to bunk down the Freedom Bus passengers for the night. I did. It was a known axiom to me that a risk such as that, possibly being censured or fired or required to pay out of my pocket the cost of such, was one that had to be taken in support of those who were taking even greater risks for change.

The same situation arose when the black college students staged sit-ins on the second Saturday of February, 1960. I was at Virginia Union University when it occurred, but I had moved to North Carolina A&T by the time the trials were held. When I learned that hundreds of my students were arrested for "sitting-in" at a segregated lunch counter to challenge the racial separation laws, I was attending a meeting of black college presidents at Princess Anne, Maryland. We were eat-

115

ing a steak lunch, complete with gold-trimmed china, linen napkins, sterling silverware, Waterford crystal, and velvet draperies securely drawn on our secret deliberations. We were preparing unified instructions for all our coaches to follow when they attended the athletic conference. In the midst of such a "profound" forum, a message came for each of us, one at a time, and we left quietly like mourners from a gravesite and with equal seriousness.

What could presidents do who were concerned but who were caught between maintaining order on their campuses and giving support to the movement? After all, colleges were important to the movement, too. All its leaders had the benefit of college training! We corralled the faculty and staff to put up deeds to their homes for bonds, spent endless hours with police chiefs to assure a nonviolent atmosphere, and secured attorneys to prepare a defense. It all worked.

A kingdom dweller does not throw Bible verses at every crisis. He or she approaches each issue, sticky, thorny, or amorphous, and looks for an approach that best promises an outcome commensurate with kingdom goals. What a terrible situation I faced when I learned that a small black college in West Virginia had closed, trustees were doing nothing to continue its program, endowment income was dwindling, and the campus growing up in weeds! It seemed tough, but the kingdom's goals were best served by salvaging those assets and putting them to use by strengthening another school—my own!—and giving that college a decent funeral. We did. We added their alumni to ours and gave their records safekeeping. We sued to annex that school to ours and won. Now *that* was walking an ethical tightrope, but it comes down to that sometimes.

I never saw a situation in which there was no way possible to function and feel compatible with the kingdom of God. Also, I have found countless unique and untried things to do to implement in marvelous ways the claims of the kingdom of God. In the midst of these radical social changes, some of us saw a need for a stronger national commitment to educate

minorities. We saw clearly the relationships between education, or the lack of it, and unemployment, crime, disease,
social disorder, and despair. We saw that new civil rights
would mean nothing without education. Black college presidents enlisted the help of well-placed leaders in education:
Jerald Zacharias of MIT, John Munro of Harvard, Logan Wilson of Texas, William Friday of Chapel Hill, Fred Harrington
of Wisconsin, Minna Reese of City University of New York,
Father Hesburg of Notre Dame, Albert Bowker of City University, Kingman Brewster of Yale, and Nathaniel Pusey of Harvard. They came forth in meeting after meeting. I recall testi-
fying before Senator Jacob Javits's committee of the Senate on
education. The room was almost empty—Senator Javits was
the only senator present, and besides myself there was a handful of reporters. I spoke as though a multitude were listening.
At one point, when I was describing the condition of some of
our students, Senator Javits began to cry.

In the end, before the decade closed, we had student loans,
Head Start, Upward Bound, work-study, and categorical
grants to black colleges. Moreover, many major universities
began to recruit black faculty to work for change from within.
In fact, I went to the University of Wisconsin at Madison with
such a commitment and returned East to Rutgers for fifteen
years with a chair in graduate education. Opportunities
abound for translating the claims of the kingdom of God into
practical applications and into lasting social change.

PASSING FROM DEATH
UNTO LIFE

There was never a time in my life when I did not believe in
immortality, the continuation of a spiritual existence after
this mortal body has ceased to function. The idea that we are
only composites of magical chemicals, with an incidental
symbiosis with nature, never found acceptance with me. I had
great difficulty with a physical heaven and hell, wondering
where they were, how they stayed put, where all of the people

who should be there found space, why a loving God would want to see anyone burned in a fire that never went out, and what kind of a God would want millions of people bowing down and praising his name every day—all day long—for ceaseless ages.

Nevertheless, I never could separate my mind from the notion that there had to be something beyond this uneven, brief, and fragmented existence to make sense of it. A just Creator would not allow this human creation to end on such a sour note after making so much harmony in nature; a loving God would not waste so much pure, human goodness in dust and ashes; and a universe shot through with meaning, coordination, and synergism would defy the idea of a human being having such a meaningless existence. So I chose to gamble on immortality. I cast my lot with Longfellow:

> Life is real! Life is earnest!
> And the grave is not its goal;
> Dust thou art, to dust returnest
> Was not spoken of the soul.[1]

Tennyson used a beautiful metaphor:

> Sunset and evening star,
> And one clear call for me!
> And may there be no moaning of the bar,
> When I put out to sea, . . .
>
> Twilight and evening bell,
> And after that the dark!
> And may there be no sadness of farewell,
> When I embark;
>
> For though from out our bourne of Time and Place
> The flood may bear me far,
> I hope to see my Pilot face to face
> When I have crossed the bar.[2]

The problem is that something as mind-stretching as the idea of immortal life will force us to invent every metaphor

1. "A Psalm of Life," stanza 2.
2. "Crossing the Bar," stanzas 1, 3, 4.

imaginable to encompass it. We will have to reach all around us looking for any image or analogy that we can find to express such an all-embracing idea. We will have to run to poetry, to drama, to myth, and to music to capture all the fullness of such an idea as immortal life. And, consequently, when one rejects this or that metaphor or this and that analogy, then the whole idea is lost or deferred indefinitely. What a temptation it is to put down the whole concept of immortality entirely when we reject a devil, with a pitchfork, throwing alcoholics, drug addicts, and car thieves into a blasting furnace. No. I have kept immortality even though the "address" has changed.

Perhaps my best understanding I learned from the First Epistle of John 3:14-15: "We know that we have passed from death into life, because we love the brethren. He that loveth not his brother abideth in death. Whosoever hateth his brother is a murderer: and ye know that no murderer hath eternal life abiding in him."

This implies that immortality begins now. It has to do with a quality of life that is more than merely breathing, sleeping, and eating. It involves the refinement of the inner life with moral coherence, selfless love, a symphony of thought and deed, and the peace and wisdom that come from communion with the living God. We live in time, but eternity impinges upon our days now, and time becomes incidental.

In terms of moral growth and development, I consider this idea the linchpin of the whole discussion. The very height of moral growth is this transcendent quality of life, beyond legalism, custom, instinct, habit, or mutual and reciprocal behavior. It is intrinsic human goodness, already passed from death into life. And this goodness is its own reward; it leads to communion with God.

This understanding of immortality derives from my faith in the perfect love of God. There are many ancient images of God—as creator, absolute ruler, lawgiver, judge and even shepherd. Jesus presented God as love. The love that Jesus spoke of was not *eros* or *philia,* but *agape,* love for the sake of the object or person loved, without thought of return, and without measuring the worth of the person loved. This love is directed toward generating good, something of worth, consequence, and benefit in the life of the one loved. It need not be a maudlin, sentimental love. It may contain chastisement, denial, discipline, or separation for the sake of the larger good. This is my understanding of the way God loves us, and with such perfect love immortal life seems like a necessary corollary.

This is the love that Jesus portrayed in the story of the prodigal son, wherein a father of patience cared deeply about restoring his lost son to the family fold. It was such love that caused Jesus to stand still on the Jericho Road when he heard blind Bartimaeus wailing, and led him to spend his nights from Palm Sunday to Maundy Thursday possibly with Simon the Leper in Bethany.

That quality of love tells me that twins born with their skulls joined together and who must spend a lifetime bent over facing the ground, who must fight their way through the gazes and stares, the giggling and thoughtless comments, and who must die together as one gives up her life when the other dies, are not going to have such courage and fortitude turn to vapor in the end. A God who loves with the love that Jesus showed to the world would make it so that the souls of persons like these twins, the part of them that never was physical, would live in a joy and a peace that they never knew in the flesh, flawed by a vagabond gene.

I saw such twins at Compton Community College in California. The president, Edison Jackson, my former student at Rutgers, and I strolled that palm-lined, sun-drenched campus on commencement day, with cameras flashing and choruses of laughter accenting the joys of accomplishment. Pastel dresses and graduation caps and gowns spread out to capture the gentle breezes. And suddenly, in my line of vision, everything ceased as I saw these Siamese twins straddling a bench, eating lunch from one plate. In a moment I followed them in my mind from the bench, to the bus, to the stairs, to the bathroom, to bed, to the study table, and back to the bus, gathering stares and hushed comments all day, every day. Indeed, a loving God knows what nature was permitted to do, in this "best possible world," and that loving God has provided immortality for these twins.

That faith, it seems to me, is one of the strongest constraints upon us when we are called upon to follow a course of high moral commitment under seriously unfair, undeserved conditions and for a full lifetime. At my fiftieth high school reunion I saw one of my old buddies with whom I spent my entire school days, from kindergarten through college. There he was, still swinging on those crutches that he had learned to live with in infancy from poliomyelitis. He had become a popular college professor and an outstanding citizen in our hometown. But all of his sixty-five years he had lived a life abbreviated and made tedious by his limitation, while many persons of sound health and mobility spent a lifetime selling drugs to destroy young lives. A loving God has an answer to that.

As I think of my friend, I am reminded of one of our teachers who played the piano very poorly but frequently volunteered anyway. She always wanted us to sing "Abide with Me" because she could play it well. When I saw my buddy with his crutches, those words came back. His hair was turning, his face was gently masked with the ripening of our years, and he moved the crutches with more deliberate paces:

> Swift to its close ebbs out life's little day.
> Earth's joys grow dim; its glories pass away.
> Change and decay in all around I see;
> O Thou who changest not, abide with me![3]

My faith in the concept of immortality derives further from my confidence in the orderliness and the teleological, i.e., "end-making" tendencies, structure and function in the universe. Nature is supportive of human existence with the water,

3. "Abide with Me," words by Henry F. Lyte, 1847.

the air, the sunlight, the reproduction, the harvests, the rain, the medicinal plants, and the mathematical consistency that allows us to send spaceships into distances we cannot even measure and have them send photographs back past the nearest stars. The natural order is so reliable that we can build sciences like physics, biology, chemistry, radiology, hematology, aeronautics, geology, and pharmacology and then publish research findings in a hundred languages, creating global fraternities of scholars relying on the same data everywhere, generation after generation.

Such order suggests that human life has far more significance than that of any other form of life and that the capacity of the brain, and our imagination, equips us for a mode of existence far different from that of dolphins, horses, and birds. For all these millions of years no other animal has built a flute, developed verbs with tenses, or cooked food. In other words, *homo sapiens* seems to have been equipped to outlive this temporal-spatial abode and, with a soul that derives from the extraordinary reflective genius of the human mind, to soar toward infinitude.

There are many forms of immortality that we could settle for and raise no argument at all. For one thing, there is the immortality one learns in building institutions and creating novelty in history. Columbus, Balboa, Hudson, Magellan, and DeSoto are all immortal insofar as their work has far outlasted their mortal abode. And even when their names are long forgotten, their contributions will echo among the canyons, oceans, and forests that witnessed their achievements.

Booker T. Washington, Sojourner Truth, and William E. B. DuBois made such indelible contributions to the progress of black people in America that when the sand erases their names from their marble monuments, generations will still be climbing higher and higher from plateaus that they made secure. That is a form of immortality.

My grandmother graduated from college in 1882, and her descendants with college degrees number over one hundred— and still counting every May! That is immortality. My great-grandfather came out of slavery as an oysterman preacher on the York River in Virginia. What on earth would he say if he saw me, his son William's daughter's son, standing in Abyssinian's pulpit on a Sunday morning, with two thousand worshipers before me and a quarter-million-dollar organ behind me!

He would surely hope that I had something useful to say, at least! Notwithstanding, old Zachariah Hughes, the Gloucester County country preacher lives in me, my sons, and his countless other heirs. That is immortality.

My brother Edgar, practicing ophthalmology, straightens the crossed eyes of little children in Atlanta. He studied medicine at Meharry Medical College, founded in Nashville, Tennessee, to train black physicians for the rural South. The Methodist ministers who founded Meharry have been dead a long time, but they live in every operation my brother performs on little children's eyes today. That is immortality.

Yet none of these kinds of immortality takes into account fully the unique status of the human mind in nature. Influence is fine, but the person himself or herself is still unaccounted for. Nature seems to be too tendentious to allow the accumulated spiritual gains of a disciplined life to evaporate at death. There seems to be a teleological necessity that cries out for a better answer. It will never be proved, I know, but one has to vote yes or no on this, and I vote yes. I believe it is important as a foundation for moral living.

My faith in immortality is based also on my conviction that God is just. There is something beautiful about a life like that of Dr. Charles Drew, the blood scientist; or John Huss, the Bohemian Bible translator; or Helen Keller, the sightless genius; or that of countless South Africans who have died in protests against apartheid; innocent, good people who have perished in the internecine strife in Ireland; or the mothers, fathers, and children who struggled against nature's whims to make a livelihood out of the meager chances in Armenia, only to have the earth divide and make a huge grave for them and 20,000 others. Yet the beauty of such lives is contradicted by the racism, physical handicaps, violent strife, and natural disasters that destroyed them.

God is just and such lives are accounted for. There are little children dying throughout the world who never had a full, hot meal or a clean drink of water. A just God is not blind to that. And as for us, it is no small thing to live out our days in a constant struggle to reconcile our desires and temptations with the moral claims of Jesus. At best we fail, but at the end of life's little day, there we are, still discontented that we missed the mark so far. We are all haunted by the words of William Cullen Bryant:

> So shalt thou rest: and what if thou withdraw
> In silence from the living, and no friend
> Take note of thy departure? All that breathe
> Will share thy destiny. The gay will laugh
> When thou art gone, the solemn brood of care
> Plod on, and each one as before will chase
> His favourite phantom; yet all these shall leave
> Their mirth and their employments, and shall come
> And make their bed with thee. As the long train
> Of ages glide away, the sons of men,
> The youth in life's green spring, and he who goes
> In the full strength of years, matron and maid,
> The speechless babe, and the grey-headed man—
> Shall one by one be gathered to thy side
> By those who in their turn shall follow them.[4]

Finally, I believe in Easter, and this is the ultimate basis for belief in immortality. I begin with Jesus as real and unique, as a special divine intervention in history. It all happened among a certain people, at a certain time, in a locus at the center of the world, Palestine. It had to be somewhere, so it was among the Roman-occupied territory of the Jews at the time of Augustus Caesar. Jesus was crucified because the Jews alleged that he accepted the identity of the Messiah of God wrongfully. Jesus had behaved contrary to their legal religious practices. He broke their "laws" as he called sinners to

4. "Thanatopsis," lines 58–72.

righteousness and initiated the spiritual kingdom of God, not the political kingdom of David.

They killed him by impaling him. The neat crosses we paint are altogether too cosmetic. Jesus died in indescribably excruciating pain. It was human cruelty at its worst, as he died with a patch of weeds slapped on his head, a spear thrust in his side, nails driven into his feet and hands, and his form impaled with a sharpened tree limb. The pain was much deeper because his friend and chief disciple, Simon Peter, lied and said that he did not know him. And another disciple, Judas, traded his life for thirty coins. Little wonder that the sun hid its face, the earth began to shake, and the rocks were split open!

He was indeed crucified. Other historians of the day testified to his crucifixion, but only the Christian sources speak of a physical resurrection, the post-resurrection appearances, and an ascension into space. All of this is a stumbling block to the twentieth-century mind that is given to scientific verification of facts, the empirical method, and unvarying, natural law. Here, again, if there is a problem with the reporting, the style of writing, the metaphors, the analogues, or the use of parable, poem, or myth to convey a spiritual truth, we are prone to throw all of it out. We need to remember that if we are dealing with a human mind receiving God's inspired Word, we may expect some human accretions to the record.

The resurrection was recorded years after the event. The church had begun, and stories of Jesus' life circulated orally. Many were rejected by the church as ill-founded. Nevertheless, there was a resurrection. Christ's presence was known. The hard facts are overwhelming. Peter who denied him took charge at Pentecost and led the new church into spiritual vitality. All the brokenhearted, confused followers of Christ came back together; sold their property and entered a close, communal life-style; and preached in his name all over the region, going into Asia Minor and Europe. Peter, John Mark, Barnabas, Mary, and John the disciple were all there in Jerusalem when it all happened. And they founded the church.

What happened exactly, how it happened, why it happened is all a mystery. That it did happen there can be no doubt. Easter was!

It has always meant to me that God gave us a sign, a strong signal, that truth crushed to earth will rise. It is the good news that although in this world we may have tribulation, Christ, for our sakes, overcame the world. It says that Pilate, Caiaphas, and the Herods of this world never have the last word. It is God's assurance that no matter what the disparities, the inequities, the unfulfilled dreams of this life may be, one day we vacate this earthly house and enter a building not made with hands, eternal in the heavens.

After many years of observing, participating, teaching, lecturing, preaching, counseling, and holding on, I have learned that the source of my strength has been that there is a God, a God who is aware of our strivings. And life does not all have to balance out here and now. The inner life is equipped for immortality.

We used to sing in Bank Street Church,

> I heard the voice of Jesus say,
> "I am this dark world's Light;
> Look unto Me, thy morn shall rise,
> And all thy day be bright."
>
> I looked to Jesus, and I found
> In him my Star, my Sun;
> And in that Light of life I'll walk
> Till trav'ling days are done.[5]

In 1962, while I was in Nigeria directing the Peace Corps, one of my finest volunteers promised me a great surprise when we visited her post. She surely did, for she carried us into a small village where I was greeted by Chief Oyrinde, a Yoruba leader with three tribal marks cut into his cheeks, deep, sparkling eyes, and a smile of real joy spread over his whole face. He was clearly pleased to see me. We acknowledged to each other that he had graduated from Virginia

5. "I Heard the Voice of Jesus Say," words by Horatius Bonar, 1846.

Union in 1911 and I in 1942. We compared notes on many mutual acquaintances, and I found that I knew a schoolmate of his named Clarence O. King of Harlem. I asked him what had he been doing for those fifty-one years, and he replied that he had been running a school, overseeing a dispensary, serving a church, and governing a village. There were no dentist, indoor toilets, MacDonalds, hospital, department store, or public high school.

Meanwhile, his schoolmate had become a prominent New York City real estate investor, treasurer of the Abyssinian Baptist Church, chairman of a bank board of directors, and had died a millionaire. He bequeathed a million dollars to our alma mater. What different sets of opportunities, life-styles, and outcomes! Why does one person have to spend an entire lifetime serving in one Yoruba village while his schoolmate lives with every convenience and comfort and becomes a millionaire? My faith in immortality tells me that Chief Oyrinde could achieve the moral and spiritual attainment of eternal life in a Yoruba village, and Clarence King could achieve the same in the fast lane of urban America. And after a while, there would be no tribal marks, skyscrapers, village well, or televisions. Both would lay down all the trappings of this world and be free for unfettered fellowship with God.

6

COPING
with My Widening World

FROM PRIVATE
TO PUBLIC MORALITY

While it was a new and exciting world that emerged for me during 1955 to 1962, compelling me to find some kind of believable and satisfying purpose in it, that same world widened further from 1962 to 1969, during seven years of more change than the human race had witnessed in the previous seven hundred. Learning to cope with such a widening world was a serious moral challenge. It all began one morning when the telephone rang. R. Sargent Shriver was calling from Washington, asking me to go to Nigeria and "launch" the Peace Corps. There was a Peace Corps on paper, in law, in embryo, but not yet kicking and breathing. There were 695 white middle-class teachers already in Africa and in trouble, largely rejected initially by curious students and suspicious militant nationalists who resented what they perceived as an invasion of an American brand of democracy and free enterprise with guitars, tennis shoes, and smiling, handshaking altruism. Their own government had indeed invited the Peace Corps and had arranged for it, but the grassroots had to be won to the idea. And that was where I, raw and uninitiated, entered.

At the first request I agreed to go. I wanted to learn more about Africa; I believed that President John Kennedy was sincerely trying to create new openings for constructive relationships among the world's most deprived and oppressed peoples; I thought that the Peace Corps was a worthwhile "for instance" of what the brightest and the best had been advocating; and, existentially, in response to a conscience furnished with the Sermon on the Mount, the Samaritan on the Jericho Road, the message of justice from the tree pruner out of Tekoa, and the struggle of blacks in America, I told him I would go.

My world began to widen. My wife and our two sons agreed to go also, and their worlds widened, too. My sons Herb and Tim integrated a "white" school in Nigeria. It seemed that from 1962 to 1969 everybody's world became wider, whether the moral capacity to cope with it was there or not. There is a stage in moral development that calls upon us to decide how we are going to view the world and the challenges presented by those unresolved issues that make the eleven o'clock news every night.

Somehow moral understanding seems to level off on a plateau at the point where we have learned to be accountable for our personal and private behavior. We become like the rich, young ruler who came to Jesus, in Luke 18:18-23, asking what was required for one to attain immortality. And when Jesus told him to keep the Commandments, he replied that he had a perfect record already. He had not stolen, murdered, committed adultery, or disrespected his parents. Big deal! Most of us have not been reckless and feckless. In private morality we all pass at least minimally. But when Jesus opened before him the wider world and asked him to consider the poor, the matter became more complicated, and he hung his head and walked away.

Beyond personal discipline and private moral accountability are those concerns that extend from personal choices, that send ripples far into wider relations that are not so readily apparent. We practice thrift and save money, but do we inquire about where our money is invested? Are we supporting discrimination against women or persons with disabilities

129

with our investments? We buy a product made abroad, and we may be supporting slave labor. The purchase of a lottery ticket may be fostering a system of supporting schools, colleges, research, and hospitals out of the pockets of the very poorest citizens, who get taxed double by this seductive scheme that exempts those most able from bearing their fair share of the load.

Without political participation we could be allowing a bribe system to drain away tax dollars to the underworld, selling guns to small nations to harass and terrorize their neighbors and leaving two-thirds of the world's children sick, hungry, and illiterate. Moreover, as we look beyond our race, class, nation, and culture, we find it disturbing to have to decide anything at all. We would rather not be bothered. We spend our moral energy trying to maintain respectability, to keep ourselves and our children inside the law, and to order our lives for mental and emotional poise and tranquility. Bad news is annoying.

Also, in order to avoid unraveling the tangled and tedious details and perhaps revealing our own complicity and guilt, we often conceal unresolved issues with simplistic, blinding slogans like "born again," "secular humanism," "strict constructionism," "reverse discrimination" and "communist threat." Such verbiage blurs the details. One must wonder why the people who use these phrases are so generally found to be supportive of private schools established to avoid integration in the public schools; they march together against equality of rights for women and affirmative action; they support high military expenditures and nuclear arms buildup; they ignore the doctrine of separation of church and state and plead for formal, sectarian prayers in the public schools.

The current issues that face us in this wider world—beyond our neat lawns, elegant churches, lush supermarkets, crowded freeways, and sun worship on hot sandy beaches— are a kaleidoscope of five billion people, speaking a thousand tongues, with a cacophony of clashing cultures that threaten to render the planet uninhabitable with one volley of nuclear explosions or the defiant spread of a stubborn AIDS virus. We would like to drop a curtain on all of it and return to our domestic preoccupations, except for the fact that those faceless billions control the world's oil; they produce magic electronic equipment that we cannot do without; they own heavy holdings in our corporations and downtown real estate; they control the worth of our dollar; many are suppliants of Soviet domination; they provide us with indispensable, critical raw material; and we need to sell them our coal, prescription drugs, farm products, and heavy machinery. Besides all of this, our own population is blood kin to most of them, all creatures of one God and made of one blood. This wider world cannot be wished away for it will not vanish.

SOURCES OF
PUBLIC MORAL ISSUES

Our problems did not spring forth full grown in the 1960s. They were the echoes of sounds begun centuries ago. I used to shock students in my college freshman class now and then by asking them to relate as many of today's social and political realities as they could to the 1600s in England—one country, one century, three hundred years ago: the founding of Jamestown, 1607; the translation of the Bible into English in 1611; the arrival of the slaves in Virginia in 1619; John Harvard's departure for Massachusetts in 1637; the execution of King Charles I in 1649; the promulgation of the Bill of Rights and the Habeas Corpus Act in England in 1689 and 1679, respectively; and John Locke's *Essay Concerning Human Understanding* published in 1690. Much of the present agitation for freedom and justice is traceable to the explosive developments of the seventeenth century, and one may say that the revolution in social and political life that began then is coming to full fruition in our own time. One may also say that the importing of slaves to America that began then caused an ugly institution to reach such massive proportions that it almost ruined this young nation; its consequences yet prevail in the vestiges of racism in our society.

Indeed, the problems of today that do abound have deeper,

ancient antecedents buried in the dusty labyrinths of history: the defeat of Darius by Alexander the Great at Issus in 333 B.C. and the opening of the Orient to the Occident; the writing of the Epistle to the Galatians by the apostle Paul, cutting the umbilical cord and separating Christianity from Judaism; the abolition of the Jewish patriarch of the Roman Empire by Theodosius II and the ostracism of Jews within Christian societies; the enslavement of young Patrick of Ireland; the victory of Saladin over the Crusaders in Jerusalem in 1187, with the loss of Palestine to the Moslems; the bloody reign of Genghis Khan in the thirteenth century; the nailing of the Ninety-five Theses on the door of the castle church at Wittenberg by Martin Luther in October of 1517; the cultivation of a taste for sugar and tea and the practices of smoking tobacco and wearing cotton; the partitioning of Africa at the Council of Berlin in 1885; the denial of Gandhi's request to ride in a "white only" car on a South African train; and the bus driver in Montgomery requiring Rosa Parks to give up her seat. This list could be much longer.

Notwithstanding the complications of tracing the roots of our problems, the moral equipment needed for making up one's mind about global matters is no different from the moral equipment needed to keep a marriage happy or to have satisfying relationships in a fraternity, a corporate board, a symphony orchestra, or a football team. Moral principles such as justice, truth, transparency, integrity, and honesty do not come in various sizes. They fit any size situation. So if one is to cope without being superficial, pretentious, evasive, or deceitful, he or she will carry into the wider world and its dilemmas, contradictions, dichotomies, and lacunal deceptions the simplicity, the sincerity, and the humility that Jesus, for example, brought to the whole human condition.

It all begins by standing tall in the full height of one's personhood, knowing first that you are somebody, with a right and an obligation to be concerned and with a share in the outcomes of all these issues. We are neither spectators nor numbers in a poll, digits on a graph, dots on a chart, or holes punched in a computer card. We are registered, warm persons. Happily, in our moral development we have cultivated the mental ability to stretch the imagination and to become empathetic and vicarious. So we can see the world through others' eyes. We have found out how to transcend prejudice and custom and to claim our own margin of freedom and license to approach issues with independent thought. We have found the principle of justice to be the key—equality of opportunity, removal of arbitrary impediments, and compensatory measures made available for undeserved, imposed deficits. We have found also that love in its highest sense, *agape*, takes the initiative to create good in the lives of others and goes beyond duty and justice. These considerations we have affirmed as we have sung to them, shaken and clapped our hands about them, written poems and plays concerning them, and lighted candles and marched in solemn procession in celebration of them. Moreover, we have surrendered our native, primordial, survival, atavistic egocentrism to One whose spirit leads us into a newness of life. And this new life is consonant with and supportive of the moral principles that we have found in our journey. We are not perfected in any of this, but through trust and faith we find forgiveness, reconciliation, and renewal. We learned not to lean on our own strength but to sing with the psalmist, "I will lift up mine eyes unto the hills, from whence cometh my help. My help cometh from the LORD, which made heaven and earth" (Psalm 121:1-2). Therefore, we do not embrace the wider world naked, alone, confused, or afraid, but poised and confident.

RECOGNIZING PERSONHOOD
IN OTHERS

The lack of sensitivity to recognize personhood in others must be one of the most glaring of human failings. The results of this failing are shameful: police abuse frightened suspects; a mother injures helpless infant children; a drug dealer sells crack to a juvenile; a judge accepts a bribe to penalize an

133

innocent person; a supervisor trades preferential treatment for sex; a strong nation terrorizes a weak state; an employer denies a job to someone because of age, race, sex, or religious affiliation. In each instance a person is reduced and manipulated, regarded as an instrument, as a means and not an end.

As we observe the swift changes that occurred in the sixties, the changes seemed to focus on the question of seeing persons as ends with innate dignity and worth. The Office of Economic Opportunity spent four billion dollars a year seeking to elevate the personhood of the nation's poorest: the quiet poor of Maine and Vermont; the lonely and hidden poor in the hollows of Kentucky and Tennessee; the forgotten poor of the Ozarks; the poor among Native Americans, Chicano farm laborers, and urban street people; the visible and angry poor of the black ghettos; the helpless, infant poor and the powerless, indigent aged. It seemed like a lot of money, but they needed everything—education, dental work, job training, housing, pride, self-respect, discipline and an affirmation of personhood. Their conditions resulted from long-term, intergenerational poverty, from nasty and contemptible racism, from an erratic economy, poor education, and family disintegration. Many seemed to have mental disorders, but there is a depth of despair and futility that looks a lot like mental illness. Many, on the other hand, believed these poor people were nobody and were trying hard to prove it.

This failure to empathize with others across class cultural and ethnic lines is so common that it passes today for politeness. We giggle at the jokes and sneers and remain so comfortable in our ignorance of the condition of others that it passes as correct behavior in sophisticated circles. It is so common that the poor laugh at jokes on themselves. They find it easy to be put down.

Once President Lyndon Johnson asked me to visit a widely acclaimed evangelist to solicit his moral support for the war on poverty. I did, and what a shock! He lived like royalty and told me that he did not get involved in such things. He only "preached the gospel." When I reminded him of what *the gos-*

pel said in Matthew 25 about feeding the hungry, giving water to the thirsty, visiting prisoners, and taking in strangers, he took refuge in some inane, insipid theological irrelevancies. Without knowing it, he dismissed Jesus as a "liberal."

As I left him, I thought of the persons who had become my saints and spiritual heroes and who had helped me to recognize personhood and dignity in others: Kagawa, who lived for the forgotten people of Japan; William Walker, who died for the cause of abolition; Gandhi, who became an untouchable for the untouchables; Saint Francis, who became poor for the poor; Father Damien, who became a leper for the lepers; Mother Teresa, mother of Calcutta's motherless; Harriet Tubman, the frail and sickly captain of the Underground Railroad for the liberation of slaves; and Rosa Parks, who laid her life across the path of history to challenge the dehumanizing practice of racial segregation. My genial host did not make that roster or come near it.

My world was widening right here in the U.S.A. I was submerged in programs and strategies that looked for ways of getting the poor out of poverty permanently. It was all new to one who had been reared to regard education as essential as breathing. I found out in Head Start, Job Corps, and Community Action programs that the poor were basically and primarily poorly educated. It meant that education took on a new significance for me, and I saw being inducted into the world of thought as *the* critical experience of living.

Beyond our shores, we need to go to the least developed countries and observe how human progress is stultified in a climate of illiteracy. It is so obvious that nations that are looking for help first need clean water, safe sewers, and good food, not rifles and tanks. And then these peoples need to be led out of superstition and fear into the life of the mind. All else is a misplaced priority. Their personhood must be recognized. This was my first moral discovery in the changing sixties. The blacks, the women, the gay community, the farm workers, the students, the poor, and the powerless were awakened to the fact that they were largely statistics and instru-

135

ments. Before answers to their *problems* could be found, *they* had to be found first as persons. This fact lay behind all the iconoclastic shaking and moving of the turbulent sixties— *persons* were crawling out of the pages of sociology texts and looking us in the face.

UNDERSTANDING INSTITUTIONAL AND CORPORATE ACCOUNTABILITY

We are so accustomed to thinking of morality as having to do with sex, alcohol, drugs, profanity, and other personal mischief that we are slow to recognize the moral accountability of trustee boards, governing boards, bureau chiefs, CEOs, newspaper editorial writers, and television programmers. As a Huntersville boy, I had a blind spot here also. I believed whatever was printed on expensive paper and gave it the benefit of all doubt. My world widened to the point of questioning all authority, especially those in all high places. More and more, as I assessed the issues of the wider world, I found that mere honesty, hard work, and faith could not mitigate the control and power of entrenched, unjust institutional and governmental policies and practices.

The most obvious case was the problem of implementing the 1954 *Brown* decision decreeing the desegregation of public schools. By 1962 very little desegregation had come about. People who were good and decent in personal matters resisted altering the life chances of blacks by removing the stigma, the negative results of separate schools, and the perpetuation of an American caste system. Persons who were "sweet" on a one-to-one basis enjoyed the anonymous existence of a wall of separation. Every item of the system of separation had to be challenged in the courts or in the streets. No major initiatives for change came from the Christian, educated, polite, civil, honorable, established leadership.

One aspect of going to Africa to direct the Peace Corps was that we needed to find a school for our young sons for the two-year term. I had learned of an excellent school in Nigeria operated by a foreign mission board in the United States, but only whites attended—in Africa! The missionaries hardly were aware that their segregated school spoke more loudly about their faith than the sermons they preached. Thankfully, however, it took only one telephone call, and a sensitive white pastor to intercede, and my sons, Herbert and Timothy, integrated the school in 1962. Institutions freeze us in some unbelievable, immoral postures.

Behind the walls of institutionalism some terribly mean measures are embraced that one would be ashamed to accept individually. In recent years a federal tax reform measure was passed by the Congress that allows persons who own homes to borrow on their accumulated home equity at 9 to 11 percent and to deduct the interest paid on these loans on their federal income tax returns. However, interest paid on exorbitant bank credit cards and department store accounts—15 to 20 percent—will no longer be deductible! So not only will homeowners get to pay lower interest, but that interest is also deductible! On the other hand, young families who are starting out and renting, the poor, the indigent aged living in subsidized housing, and the workers who receive nominal and low wages all cannot buy homes at all, yet pay the *highest credit costs* and cannot deduct it on their taxes! The persons who thought of that tax law probably go to churches, have university degrees, and have taken solemn pledges about justice, love, and brotherhood. This is that wider world, the world beyond the dining room table and the "chaney ball" tree. Moral growth requires that one confront institutions by using the means available and hold them accountable.

When the war on poverty funded tenants' groups to challenge landlords who violated their rights, we learned that one group in a large urban center caused an embarrassment because the landlord being challenged in that city happened to be a major contributor and leader in the political party in power. The tenants' group consequently had to choose a less troublesome target. This is that wider world that I found with my naive, simplistic idealism. Moral growth brings us to the awareness that moral accountability is often deceptively masked with honorable and respectable labels; yet we are obliged to live with this awareness and to probe beneath such institutional veneer to seek for moral decency.

VIGILANCE AND MORAL LEADERSHIP

In recent years our nation was shocked by three revelations: (1) A leading, married aspirant for the presidency was accused of having an affair with a young model, leaving thousands of stunned supporters shaking their heads; (2) two popular television preachers were forced off the air, following press revelations of indiscretions and marital infidelity; and (3) a paragovernment was operating in the White House and making deals with nation-states without the knowledge or consent of the congress, the president, or the responsible cabinet officers. Furthermore, files of the details of this paragovernment were shredded to avoid any full reconstruction of events and details, with the alleged consent of the Justice Department.

Every generation has its share of scandals, but the dimensions of these three were rather gross. On the one hand, they speak to the need for vigilant, courageous journalism with freedom to tell the truth. And they speak to the need for disciplined moral leadership. Leaving my neat little world of educational pursuits, career escalation, personal success, and service, it was not easy to learn that the wider world was filled with such glaring moral ambiguity, compromise, and self-serving mendacity. Sound moral development must leave room for such, and one has to learn to cope with this in the wider world, beyond Huntersville with its fig bushes, ice wagons, and fresh fish.

Many years ago, Lord Acton said, "Power corrupts; absolute power corrupts absolutely." Indeed, such a tendency is the reason why vigilance is so critical, for power continues to corrupt absolutely. Persons must undergo a moral transformation whereby those genetic, glandular, libidinal, egocentric drives and urges, the atavistic proneness to seize and to cling to a known advantage, and the lure toward hubris and wanton self-aggrandizement become harnessed, tamed, bridled, and successfully sublimated and redirected. It is like Saul of Tarsus becoming Paul the apostle when a blinding light knocked him from his horse on the Damascus Road. Ours may not be nearly as dramatic, but whenever such a rebirth to a new value system has not taken place, we may expect devious and malevolent behavior. It is not always apparent because it is often cloaked in respectability, zeal, and high endeavor.

Obviously not everyone occupies a position of leadership or is in a place where his or her voice can be heard. This means that we have to support those agencies and organizations that do represent our concerns, even if not *all* of our concerns and even if they represent other concerns not yet high on our list. This is not easy, but it is all we have. It means also supporting advocates and political candidates whose moral outlook and temperament best correspond to what we regard as vigilance and moral leadership.

NOVELTY VERSUS TRADITION

Obviously, not all things that are new and untried are good. In my neighborhood persons were always quoting aphorisms that capsuled significant ideas, although the ideas so conveyed still had to be tested. One was

> Never be the first,
> the new to be tried;
> Nor the last to
> put the old aside.

It was a caution to find the safe middle and to be sure to remain right there. This, of course, suggests that there is no way to test the new by any rule except its "newness." Yet we all know that some of the finest human developments—the incandescent lamp, typhoid vaccinations, indoor toilets, and the pneumatic tire—were all *once* sheer novelty. Our problem is not with novelty, however, but in shattering old, immoral arrangements among persons and nations. It is more a problem of blind and mindless traditionalism that gives sanctity and respectability to unfair and destructive customs, habits, and precedents. In the period 1962 to 1969, the world and our country by virtue of its world leadership were compelled to reexamine a great many of its hoary assumptions.

In 1968 I was asked to join a group traveling with Vice-President Hubert H. Humphrey to Africa. Because I had worked in Africa, I was chosen—I suppose—and it seemed wise to have blacks escort American high officials on such trips. Associate Justice Thurgood Marshall of the Supreme Court was on Air Force II for this junket also. There were aboard the typical sounds of loud discussion and debates about everything from Vietnam, the New York Mets, Castro, and failing schools to the revolt of women, rock music, and the stock market. We swept swiftly through contemporary Americana—cash laden, leisure loving, overweight, hypertensive and guilt-ridden—and landed in Africa.

In each country we found ourselves moving among members of the oligarchy, plutocratic and ruthlessly absolute, abounding in boring luxury, jewelry, rituals, and senseless protocol and clinging to the remnants of colonial thinking and behaving. They all seemed not to notice students in revolt, radical slogans painted on the corrugated tin walls, schoolboys glued to transistor radios, and peasants taking longer and longer to get out of the path of Peugeots, Mercedes-Benzes, Rovers, and Cadillacs. Resentment of the ruling class was as obvious as the stench from moldy garbage, open sewers, and street urine. Likewise, the remnants of an evil, destructive, callous, and dehumanizing order that had lasted for centuries were conspicuously apparent.

Everywhere we went, in eight countries, we were welcomed with steak, scotch, and caviar by the oligarchy and ignored or treated with contempt by students and street people. The message was deafening. It seemed like fun to fly with such interesting people, but I wished we could have remained airborne! We had no real response to the hopeless gap between our hosts and the people over whom they ruled.

Vice-President Humphrey was made aware of this when students at Addis Ababa stormed his procession and threatened to get to him. Another time the leader of one country wanted us to tour his *twelve* palaces! The irrelevance of the leaders of those states in 1968 was a convincing portent of what was to follow. And our irrelevance on such a trip was equally incongruous. We seemed to be celebrating a system of shame.

European colonialism had reduced the peoples of Africa to a dehumanized mass of subservience, and tolerance of it was clearly over. The blacks had had it, and the rulers who were not responsive had had it, too, and did not know it. We were locked into the same tradition, treating people like heaps when they were persons. It was time for novelty, something entirely new to rectify old wrongs and to begin to restore and to redeem.

Novelty is risky and scary, but "traditionalism" in dealing with this widening world is useless. Trying to force democracy, the Bill of Rights, and free elections on people with no education and no clean water is futile. Trying to compel all our friends to embrace our form of capitalism when people live on three hundred dollars a year is a vain illusion. There must be something between slavery and Wall Street, something between "Baby Doc" Duvalier and communism! But here we are, leaving young nations to flounder, to be ridiculed, and end up in the Soviet orbit. Then come the "freedom" lovers with tanks, guns, and Oliver North. We need something new that reckons immediately with poverty and illiteracy but which also protects freedom and dignity while social and economic amelioration takes place, using strategies that are compatible with the situation facing those we aim to help.

It is nothing new to cling to old despots who have been

rejected by history and who have no other country but ours where their planes can land when they flee their own nations. It is nothing new to bomb Libyan women and children in their sleep. "Conservatism" in dealing with unfair and inhuman arrangements among our own people, and those around the world, is often a euphemism for injustice and callousness. It is safe and pleasant to those not victimized, but moral maturity compels us to examine such arrangements in the light of justice and accountability. In the wider world, with its enormous speed, size, and power, there is still no exemption from honest, sincere, moral accountability. It is still amazing how the name of Jesus—with his eleven illiterate supporters, having no friends, no money, no guns, and no political power—became the noblest and most enduring name in the world, even though he was crucified in an isolated corner of the world under a puppet ruler and with the permission of a Roman proconsul in a desolate post. The rightness of his cause supplanted all the august pomp and power of the Caesars. Faith in this reality gives us a moral perspective and the personal confidence in coping with the issues in the wider world.

7

PURSUING

Genuine Community

I began these past twenty years in a maelstrom of social revolution in America. College students were resisting the nation's involvement in Vietnam. While I was an administrative officer at the University of Wisconsin, we were embattled further by the demands of alienated black students who had been recruited from Chicago and Milwaukee and who were estranged by the chill of a campus of largely midwestern "farm products." Buildings were occupied by protesting students on campuses all over America; and the Ohio National Guard had shot into a protesting student gathering at Kent State University, resulting in fatalities that shocked the nation. At the University of Wisconsin at Madison a researcher in a science building died when the building was bombed. Women resisted the image of being a "cute mom" in the kitchen, who was barefoot and pregnant—and uninformed. Mexican farm workers were in revolt, and the Democrats had lost the White House to Richard Milhous Nixon and Spiro Agnew.

Having become accustomed to crisis thinking, with constant practice since 1955, I trained my eyes to look for the important and the enduring aspects of each situation. It was my habit to be deliberative, to weigh and to measure, to defuse the rhetoric, and to try to think things through. I was reaching fifty and very much aware of the passing of time. The days were getting precious. I found myself remembering the lines of that famous poem:

> Grow old along with me!
> The best is yet to be,
> The last of life, for which the first was made:
> Our times are in his hand
> Who saith, "A whole I planned,
> Youth shows but half; trust God; see all,
> nor be afraid!"[1]

I came to Rutgers in March, 1969, with a very special set of circumstances. At Wisconsin, after six months, it was clear that my mission was aborted. I had gone there, among other things, to create a Big Ten university base for gathering funds and recruiting strong prospects to prepare for teaching in the black colleges of the South. This had begun already on a sporadic basis, and it was about to proceed. Schools like the universities of Illinois, Minnesota, Iowa, Iowa State, Purdue, Indiana, Michigan, Michigan State, and others were thinking of a consortium, each with a chosen specialty, to create a stream of bright young Ph.D.s to revitalize academic excellence in one hundred black colleges. But the rebellions on campuses deferred all this.

Harvard's Dean Elder had invited me to consider coming there to do much the same thing on a more modest scale, with Harvard doing it *sui generis*—a class by itself! And I had decided to, but had not actually signed up. I had learned from previous experience to "sleep on it." On my way from Harvard Square back to Madison, I stopped at Rutgers to give an address in memory of Martin Luther King, Jr., on the first birthday celebration since his assassination in April of 1968. I spoke to a fairly full assembly in the chapel at Rutgers, and on the back row sat James Wheeler, department chairman of educational foundations in the Graduate School of Education; Milton Schwebel, the dean of that school; Richard Schlatter, an erudite historian who was the provost (grand "high-

1. Robert Browning, "Rabbi Ben Ezra," stanza 1.

cockalorum"!), and Mason Gross, the genial, self-possessed, aristocratic president. They offered me a professorship with a tidy salary, tenure, and the Martin Luther King, Jr., Memorial Chair.

When I reached the airport at Madison, with offers from Harvard and Rutgers in my pocket and with Wisconsin on fire, my wife and I were speechless. At this time our family had grown to four sons, and everyone was excited. Imagine, the shoeshine boy from the naval base gate wiring Harvard to decline a deanship! Harvard, *sui generis!* It was tough to do, but I traded a leather chair and an oak desk for the dynamic interchange of the classroom. I was dripping with ideas that had filled my cup while administering in colleges, the Peace Corps, the National Council of Churches, the Office of Economic Opportunity, and the Institute for Services to Education. From 1964 to 1969 I had been changing hats in fairly rapid succession, keeping pace with the changes in the country at large. The residue, however, was a fund of observations and conclusions waiting for a captive audience, namely, the classroom.

In addition to all this, another activity that had begun in the 1950s had now accelerated generously. I had found a pleasant reception in the college chapels around the East—at Duke, Princeton, Penn State, Bucknell, Lycoming, Muhlenberg, Dickinson, Albright, Lehigh, Howard, Hampton, Dillard, Southern, Morehouse, Bennett, Lincoln, Coe, Ottawa, Smith, Mount Holyoke, Vassar, Wellesley, Cornell, Dartmouth, Middlebury, Boston University, Harvard, Brown, Claremont, and about. Pastors' conferences at Stetson, Furman, Richmond, and Wake Forest had received me well. When William Coffin went to Vietnam for six weeks, he asked me to keep the chapel at Yale in his absence. One cannot watch such a development in a career without giving close heed to the implications. It was clear that I had a responsibility.

There were many voices of change speaking but not all in one accord. Many voices had given up on America as a capitalist monster stalking the earth with nuclear threats, hopelessly intractable. There was an "underground" preparing for insurrection from beneath and within. Many black voices assailed the racism, the hypocrisy, and the adamant resistance to justice. They were willing to pay any price to voice their indignation and vent their frustration. Women's groups were protesting intransigent male chauvinism. The homosexual community had come "out of the closet" and wanted to be heard and seen. Every time I put on my gown and hood and approached a microphone, I knew that my audience included this entire spectrum of views on change in America. In addition to these, we had white supremacists fighting school integration, the right-wing group screaming against gun control and abortions, and the "fundamentalists" pleading for prayer in public schools and tax exemption for segregated schools "in the name" of Jesus.

Nevertheless, when the time comes for one to enter the homestretch of his or her career, that magic midpoint with twenty years *done* and twenty *to go,* it should be decided by then how this task of living a moral life should be attempted. And I was committed to spend my energies in pursuit of a genuine community in America and in the world. And, fortunately in all of this, I could count on the backing of my wife Bessie and our four sons, Herb, Tim, Sam, and Steven. The polarization, extremism, and intense belligerence that we saw on television each night found me dauntlessly convinced that America, with all of its problems and uneven progress, was still the hope of the world. No other nation comprised such variety and pluralism, such freedom and democratic institutions of government, and such abundant resources. If there were to be any place at all where a genuine community could find an incubator, it should be among America's ethnic masses living in freedom and democracy.

I preached the same message in Riverside Church in New York City and at the black First Baptist Church in Nashville, Tennessee; to black students at Florida A & M in Tallahassee and to white students at Brown. In fact, I was convinced that we had already seen such a movement toward community begin, if albeit far too slowly. I had lived thirty-three years of

146

my life under the Supreme Court's Plessy-Furguson decision that allowed states to bar me from libraries, museums, rest rooms, theatres, and hospitals. But I had seen that same court reverse all of that in 1954. I had seen mentally retarded children who were once left tied, yelling and dirty, to tree stumps with impunity to their parents and others, transported to clean schools to be taught by the highest-paid teachers in town. I had seen Social Security established and the fortunes of the elderly changed. I had seen Lyndon Johnson, a Texas politician, team up with Adam Clayton Powell, Jr., the dynamic preacher-congressman from Harlem, and pilot sixty-seven pieces of socially redeeming legislation through the congress. I had seen a black senator elected from Massachusetts and the chief NAACP attorney named to the Supreme Court. On the world scene, Mahatma Gandhi had taken a goat and a stick, with nonviolent resistance, and caused the British fleet to weigh anchor in the Bay of Bengal and sail home to Liverpool. So in my mind I had an arsenal of evidence that change was possible, and in my heart there was the flame of desire to work for the success of the American promise made in the Declaration of Independence and the Preamble to the Constitution:

> We hold these truths to be self-evident, that all men are created equal, that they are endowed by their Creator with certain un-alienable Rights, that among these are Life, Liberty and the pursuit of Happiness.

> We the People of the United States, in Order to form a more perfect Union, establish Justice, insure domestic Tranquillity, provide for the common defence, promote the general Welfare, and secure the Blessings of Liberty to ourselves and our Posterity, do ordain and establish this Constitution for the United States of America.

THE NATURE OF
GENUINE COMMUNITY

Genuine community is perhaps more readily understood when we compare it with a kind of community that is more superficial than genuine. For example, every weekend in the

147

fall and winter we gather by the millions before television screens and in our massive athletic stadiums and arenas to witness our favorite teams in combat. It is common to see thousands of white fans fanatically cheering at a basketball game with ten black players knocking each other down. Those throngs look like the signs of community. They transcend race, class, and national origin. But the whole purpose of their togetherness is far too trivial to be called community.

All of us belong to some form of community that is a facsimile of the larger national community for which we strive. I recall that when Moms Mabley became seriously ill, I found out that she was a member of our church, Abyssinian in Harlem. By then Adam C. Powell, Jr., had died, and I had become the pastor. A large urban church is hardly ever aware of its full membership. Comedians, professional ball players, and band leaders are not regular in attendance. Moms Mabley was well up in years but still doing her act, dressed like a poor street beggar, disheveled and unkempt, and making jokes on the poor, old men, old women, sexual impotency, and physical unattractiveness. At her funeral the church was filled with comedians—Flip Wilson, Dick Gregory, Bill Cosby, "Slappy" White, and the whole gang. Word had gotten around. Under one roof were most persons who made prosperous careers from comedy. And they comprised a community.

When Count Basie, the inimitable jazz band leader died, his funeral was at our church, also. In college I had earned much of my fees by playing saxophone in a student jazz orchestra with the famous pianist Billy Taylor, a fellow student at Virginia State College, as our accompanist, and we played Count Basie's "One O'Clock Jump" three or four times a night by popular demand. I felt so privileged, as a minister fifty years later, delivering his eulogy. In the church were over two thousand jazz musicians and Basie fans. Joe Williams, the loose-moving, brass-throated blues singer, came to the pulpit rostrum and sang Duke Ellington's "Come Sunday," moving everyone to tears. Speaking of community, one could hardly expect ever to see a group so agglutinated for a ninety-minute funeral. But when they left, that community that they celebrated so briefly practically dissolved.

Community is the experience of persons drawn together as subscribers to certain basic values that they all embrace. When these values are surface, relatively temporary, and inconsequential, such as fans of the same team or lovers of the same "rock" artist, it may be community, in some sense like Elvis Presley idolaters, but it falls short of what I call *genuine* community. The word "genuine" is used to suggest depth, reaching deeper into life's principal functions and concerns; it refers to durability, spanning generations and centuries; and it refers to breadth, having the capacity to reach beyond one's own clan and culture and embrace ever-widening circles of humanity.

Under President Jimmy Carter, when I served on a committee to give oversight to recombinant DNA research, I found that scientists of the world were in community. Often when we found an experiment too risky for our regulations, we would learn that it was being conducted somewhere else in the world. And how did we know? The scientists all knew one another at that level. They talked across continents on the telephone. That is an extremely meaningful community, but it excludes ballet dancers, house painters, history teachers, and rabbis. It is not inclusive enough.

My moral understanding culminates with a commitment to a kind of community that builds on acknowledging one another's total personhood, looking upon persons as equal to ourselves and not as our pawns or instruments of our designs. Each person is endowed with rights that are inherent and with worth that is conferred by God, our Creator. The immediate conditions of their lives do not diminish their worth or render them any less significant as persons. Anyone who saw Booker T. Washington, a young ex-slave walking barefoot through the thickets on the top of the Blue Ridge Mountains trying to get to Hampton Institute, would never have dreamed that one day he would dine at the White House with the president of the United States and with the king and queen of England in Buckingham Palace.

Such a community rests also on the premise that all the arbitrary and undeserved impediments to one's development and human fulfillment should be removed, and community is enriched as we pursue this goal. This includes political action and economic programs designed to remove such impediments. A further premise of this genuine community is that those of us who have *inherited* opportunities and sponsorship that we *never deserved* or *earned* are morally bound to enable those who *inherited* disadvantages and obstacles that they did not *deserve* or *earn* to achieve the same outcomes that we are enabled to achieve, with our *unearned* and *undeserved* opportunities and sponsorship.

No one can do that alone. But in genuine community it becomes a basis of our common striving. No one nation or society can achieve such a community in one generation, but it can move in that direction. In a war-weary world, with regional skirmishes in the Middle East, Ethiopia, Nicaragua, Korea, Somalia, South Africa, and the Philippines, such a community is remote but worth moving toward. If this idea of community is not clear or if it seems too idealistic, imagine what would be the *opposite* to it: we would do all that we could to guarantee that those born with *unearned* and *undeserved* impediments should *never* be assisted in overcoming such impediments, lest they should end up achieving what we have achieved with our unearned and undeserved advantages.

Clearly, this sense of community that I have advocated has not been popular. Those who have advocated such have been stoned, martyred, led to the gallows and to the crosses of history. And the world is still in confusion; hunger and death hover over the majority of the earth's people; the hot breath of revolution and violence breathes on us from three continents; and it takes one-half of our national income to buy guns to protect ourselves. So if this definition of genuine community seems unrealistic, where have we gotten with other programs of competition, mutual suspicion, grudging Darwinism, and idolatrous super-patriotism? This concept of genuine community, or something near it, must occupy the summit of any scale of moral behavior.

THE MICROCOSM OF
GENUINE COMMUNITY:
THE FAMILY

Genuine community is first learned in the primary community of the family. In the commercially driven, hedonistic rat race that we have allowed our society to become, the home for us is merely a "pit stop." We rush in to change our oil, check our tires, replace our fuses, stock up with gas, and head back for the track. We leave home in the dark to allow time required to be parked in traffic on the freeway—one person per Taurus; and we return home at night in time to kiss the kids before they fall asleep. On Saturday we shop for bargains at the mall or for a new "pit" and drink beer while watching a ball game or two. So the family may ripen or not while we are not even looking. On the contrary, a precious few are involved in moral discoveries with the family as the laboratory of living human specimens.

Ideally, the family should be the microcosm of genuine community. This is the primary unit within which life begins and values begin to be defined. The family is not always what it was. Thirty-seven percent of children born today, 1989, are born into nonnuclear, nontraditional family structures. Fortunately, it does not mean that their experience of family is always negative. We know now that poverty, not negligence or the lack of love, is the main problem of single-parent families. Obviously, if both parents bring assets to the rearing of children, the burden should lessen on both.

My father and mother were as old-fashioned as flatirons, oil lamps, and graphophones. They were not always in agreement, but Mamma ran the house and Daddy "brought home the bacon." We learned to have regard for each sibling and to show respect to any elders who joined our household from time to time. And the interest that our parents took in our schoolwork, our music, our plays, and our projects—all six of us!—has carried over into our generation.

Children learn what is important by what adults accentuate; and when we show interest in books and ideas, in physical

151

health and development, and in treating persons as ends and not as means, children learn all of that. I will never forget how I quit smoking. I began smoking in college, in order to look mature. In Virginia using tobacco was loyalty to the economy. On a big football Saturday, with two games on at once, I asked my eight-year-old Samuel what he wanted. It was after much travel and absence from home; so I had told him that it was his day. He could have anything if it cost no money and if I did not have to go out. It was frigid outside.

He said, "I only want two televisions downstairs to watch both games at once, and no smoking!" Well, after years of nursing cigarettes, I thought this was ridiculous. Quit with an hour's notice? But I asked him to get an alarm clock. We set it at three-hour intervals. Every time it rang we advanced it. I was quitting smoking in three-hour segments. By noon I was eating peelings, seeds, and leaves! I struggled, while he stood watching with his full, round head, wide eyes, rabbit teeth, and fat knees rubbing each other in thick corduroy pants. I was in agony. By nine P.M. I gave up and went to bed. I dreamed of smoking all night long. I had wanted to quit but never could find the discipline. But when my son told me that he wanted me to *live,* long before it was popular to quit, I felt terrible about smoking; and I gave it up, cold turkey, in one day. This is the kind of thing that passes from parent to child and child to parent when things are going well in the family. God grant it to all families!

The recognition of personhood causes generational walls to seem invisible. For ten years my two young sons, Steven and Samuel, and I were locked into a floating bowling tournament. We have books with ten years of scores, from the youngest at age seven till he was seventeen. We bowled everywhere we went. The older of the two was captain of his high school team, Central Jersey champions, averaging 184! And I learned to beat him in fierce, sweaty, exhausting competition. He and I traveled together to New Zealand in 1974 when I had a three-week tour with the ministry of education there. On the way home we stopped in Honolulu. After touring the main island one day, we spent the entire second day in a bowling alley! The age barrier vanished.

For thirteen years we had a small cinder block cabin on the shore of the Chesapeake Bay, where eight families had bought the edge of a farm and created a colony, largely for children. We fished; crabbed; swam; water-skied; played pinochle, football, and baseball; told long stories; and ate ourselves into bad health. It was an experience in "childfare." All things involved children, and what a joy to see them find their way into the world of words, ideas, and facts under the gentlest and warmest sponsorship! One does not need to be in a cabin on the bay for that experience. Such involvement takes place now in a housing project tenement and on a Missouri farm. Here is where we learn to become a subscriber to genuine community.

We learned that the interest of one is the interest of all, that what puts the family over puts us all over. We learned to enjoy each other's successes, and that, too, carried over into adulthood. When my youngest brother, Edgar, the Atlanta physician, announced to us that he wanted to return to college, at age twenty-nine with a wife and two sons, and go straight through to the M.D. degree, the other five of us found our assignments. Oliver, the dentist, paid his rent and utilities; Daddy gave him a used car, a little better than the one he himself had; Charles paid his Sears bill each month—if Sears did not sell it, Edgar did not need it! And I paid for his tuition and books. Harriett and Vernon sent spending change, and Ed earned his food and incidentals as a night janitor in a large church on the boulevard. It all seemed quite natural.

This family unit follows us into all dimensions of life, our successes and our failures, marriages, job searches, transfers, illnesses and college and graduate degrees. When my second son, Timothy, finished law school at Chicago and found a very good position with a major corporation in New York, he then began a "wife search." All of us were invited to comment on the prospects, but he was moving much too slowly and adding more prospects all the time. One day a jewel came to my office,

153

sent by her pastor because a certain professor kept paying her too much attention. She wanted a way to turn him away without failing his course. She was gracious, not haughty or self-righteous, concerned but not crusading, terribly good-looking but modest. I thought of our Timothy. I advised her to accept the professor's next invitation to lunch and to bring her boyfriend along. She said that at the moment she had no boyfriend. Well, she and our Timothy have been married for ten years and have two fine children, our little Katie and David. In community we seek the best for one another, starting in the family.

My oldest son, Herb, kept complaining that he could not find friends his age with his interests. I learned about the North Jersey Philharmonic Glee Club. He made contact, and he sings bass with this unusual group of men. Their concerts in New Jersey and New York are among the finest offerings we have. He loves it. It does not matter that his father made the contact; he benefits, and community is fulfilled further in the family network. I have been at Rutgers for nearly twenty years, and since I have been here eight members of my family have earned degrees, including our sons Herbert and Steven, two doctorates, my nephew Ronald, his wife, Sandra, and a third, our Sam, in the pipeline. Community, as known in the family percolates and spills over into all aspects of our lives as we engage in the constant pursuit of a shared set of values.

At the center of this is my wife, Bessie, who is the "inspector general." Although she was trained as a teacher, my activities and those of our four active sons robbed her of a chance to follow a "career," and homemaking has been her calling. For all these years we have managed our limited finances on a mutual respect basis, and she has always had her own "budget." It has grown as our fortunes changed, and she handles her own bills and her own modest checking account. Her car is in *her* name! In other words, the wife and mother is unquestionably a standup participant in all decisions. I never believed that women's liberation required anything more than regarding women as total persons with total fairness. Because

my wife has managed the home, as I earned, our future planning cares for her at my death as though she had been the
principal earner all the time. This takes no special charity or
nobility. It simply is fair. And fairness is a principal basis for
community. Family should never be an exemption from fairness, a quiet, hidden asylum for an abusive relationship for
anyone. It should be the widest portal on the outside world,
a place where we retreat from the battles of life and return
refreshed and restored.

Marriage is a voluntary association in which neither person
is the other's property. It is a microcosmic application of that
broad range of interpersonal skills of acceptance, negotiation,
compromise, and mutual trust. When it is successfully exe-
cuted, marriage becomes one of the best examples of the concept of genuine community, the sharing of salient values. And,
persons who marry should have some knowledge of the value
system to which the other subscribes, before the ceremony,
when something can be done about it.

THE HEALING IN
GENUINE COMMUNITY

Community requires us to ease the suffering of those who are
most victimized, whoever and wherever they are. The fact
about life is that it involves a considerable amount of pain.
Lots of people hurt at anytime, everywhere. The New Testament seems to spend a great deal of time talking about the
sick, the abused, and the forgotten people. The great prophets
of the eighth century B.C. in Israel were involved with the
suffering of the poor and the oppressed.

One of our obvious failings in America is our inability to
maintain our high standard of living without the concomitant
of so many, many more persons living like scavengers. So if
community means persons joined together by virtue of shared
values, rather than living in belligerence and estrangement,
there can be no community with the present disparities. The
guilt feelings that we have are fully deserved because we have

155

been geniuses at figuring out how to live in nice homes, eat good food, sleep and ride in great comfort, but absolute failures in helping others to find minimal food, clothing, and shelter. Any discussion of the moral requirement to pursue community must begin here.

When Jesus and his disciples left the Mount of Transfiguration, where they tasted a moment of eternity dipped into time, the ethereal bliss of that divine interlude was still lingering when a man brought to them his son, foaming at the mouth, gnashing with his teeth and running uncontrolled into the water and the fire. Community must begin with healing the hurt people of the world.

As I consider the experiences of these past twenty years, at the crest of my career, I thank God that Dr. James Mac-Cracken sought me out to serve on the board of the Christian Children's Fund. Quite frankly, before joining them, I felt, like so many others, that these organizations spent so much time soliciting funds that they could not be doing much for children. Well, what a revelation! Here this organization is, with a handsome building in Richmond, the workday beginning with prayer and group worship, a beautifully integrated staff of pleasant people, the very highest-quality leadership of each division, and an ecumenical board of directors that rivals any I have seen in forty years. It is an education to sit at its two-day meetings. In twenty-seven regional offices scattered around the globe, we service 500,000 of the world's poorest children with schooling, clothes, health care, and family counseling. We spend religiously only 20 percent of all funds raised on fund raising and administration, and 80 percent goes directly into the education and health care of the world's poorest and sickest children.

On our board of directors is a young Chinese physician from California who studied medicine at the Medical College of Virginia. His value to us is inestimable because the Christian Children's Fund found him in his early childhood, a street child in Hong Kong, eating wherever he found food. On my wall in my study is the picture of a Muslim student in a Roman

Catholic primary school in The Gambia, West Africa. Our family supports this young African schoolboy through monthly contributions to the Christian Children's Fund. He is a Muslim in a Catholic school in Africa; we are black Baptists from Virginia. Genuine community is real when it reaches out to heal. We have only begun to understand the world's pain and the urgency of responding to it.

The Abyssinian Baptist Church was founded in 1808, when Thomas Jefferson was president, in the same way that most historic black churches began. Segregated worship insulted black Christians and forced them to withdraw to save their honor. Just as the black church began to assert the dignity of all God's people, so the black church has had to be the unmuffled voice of social redemption in America across the years. The black church was the cradle for both the black colleges and the civil rights movement. But today the black church broods over the agony in our ghettos with dismay.

In 1972 Adam Clayton Powell, Jr., died after a career of outstanding productivity both as pastor of the Abyssinian Baptist Church in New York City and as the United States congressman from Harlem. His advocacy of the cause of the poor and the deprived led him into storms of controversy. However, his trademark was his passion for justice and his concern for neglected people everywhere. I succeeded him and served the church while I also taught at Rutgers University. Under ordinary circumstances that would have been totally unacceptable, but the church felt that I was needed especially at the time and I accepted. Since I was teaching and dividing my time with the church, I refused to accept the pastor's salary but divided it among able assistants: William Epps, Marvin McMickle, Calvin Butts, Marvin Bentley, Sharon Williams, James Curenton, Derrick Harkins, and Dino Woodward. They served successively and some have moved on to lead some of the strongest congregations in America.

This church has had a ministry of bringing persons to wholeness in one of the most troubled communities in our country. Much time is spent with victims of drug addiction,

157

unemployment, poor housing, mental illness, alcoholism, family disintegration, poor education and counseling, chronic illnesses, and abandonment. When persons visit our services and observe us in our doctoral gowns; rejoice to the music of our great choirs under Dr. Jewel Thompson and Thomas Riggsby; hear our sixty-seven-rank, five-manual Shantz organ played masterfully by Dina Foster; and observe dozens of visitors from Europe, Asia, Africa, the Pacific, and the Caribbean; they seem to think that this is "it." But before the echo of the organ dies down and I can change my wet shirt, there is a line formed at the door to the minister's study. Every other person in the line hurts, somehow. Yet, every *other* person has brought to the church extraordinary strength and resources of education, talent, experience, and commitment to Christ.

Dr. Adam Clayton Powell, Sr., pastor from 1908 to 1948, and Adam Clayton Powell, Jr., created an expectation among the people that the church was the healing agent and that we had some kind of answer to every crisis. And we labor with the conviction that this is our calling in ministry—to be the voice, the eyes, the hands, and the feet of Jesus in this present world. It has been a royal privilege to lose myself in the service of Abyssinian for seventeen years, with the most dedicated colleagues one could ask for. The task is endless. We are now building housing for senior citizens and renovating spent and worn apartments for the homeless, but it seems like such a small thing compared to the need. All over America we see how far we must go to achieve genuine community, beginning with the hungry, the homeless, the hurting people of our land.

Churches exist in a social context, never in a vacuum. So some of our white, suburban congregations reflect the affluence, the indifference, and the smugness of America's upper class. Likewise, blacks who have harnessed themselves with education, pride, discipline, and ambition have found themselves clustering in black middle-class churches. And the masses are not interested in fellowship with them. The worship styles are different. The training of the pastors and leaders is different. The use of the English language is different. Hence, the churches with the strong role models and the resources are inhibited in their access to the persons whose lives are most troubled: the poorly educated, the underemployed, the street "crack" dealer, and the mothers who are still children themselves.

The values cherished most are the most difficult to transpose into meaningful social articulation in a society as classbound as ours. It is a real test of our political will because we are committed to freedom, not a benevolent dictator. In Cuba, the Soviet Union, or China, there are answers that are not acceptable to us. Therefore, the concerns of our churches and synagogues, our mosques and temples must somehow be translated into meaningful ways of relieving the pain of our time on a voluntary basis.

Unfortunately, the greatest pain may be felt by those who are most despised among us, namely the young middle-class drug user, bored with having so much without working; and the poor ghetto drug addict who never had anything. On the one hand are the tough-minded, successful, hard-driving, "realistic," "practical," fathers, husbands, merchants, politicians, and readers of *Time, Forbes, Barron's, Newsweek,* and the *Wall Street Journal;* they cannot understand how they could begin life as a paperboy and end up with an MBA, living in Westchester, with a six-figure income and a boat. On the other are these "humanoids" (as one New York radio host calls them) who cannot stay aware and alert long enough to figure things out. It will call for the utmost of intelligence, compassion, and commitment for the strong, in this instance, to bear the infirmities of the weak and not settle for jailing and "warehousing" our young who have escaped into drugs. Instead, we have to find the means of reaching them and helping them to find the life abundant.

COMMUNITY AND THE ALTERING
OF LIFE CHANCES

Community further requires us to alter substantially the life chances for those who are most disadvantaged. I suppose that as one who has been engaged in education and ministering in the church, I have had this particular challenge engage me more than any other need. Throughout these seven segments of my life, my moral odyssey, I have reported on the levels of moral challenge to which I felt myself attempting to respond. Obviously, it is not the case that I have felt victorious at any stage but, rather, that I have been aware of the continuing opportunity for moral growth. Here we are now at the seventh stage of the journey, the pursuit of genuine community. No stage has been more crucial to me, and none has been so frustrating. We may not find it easy to effect community, but each of us can "live it" wherever we are, despite the frustrations we may experience.

While at Rutgers from 1969 to 1984—and still teaching a course there in 1988—I have had an excellent opportunity to function on the growing edge of community. It is a university of 47,000 students and over 5,000 faculty, at the halfway point between Washington and Boston and between Philadelphia and New York, and on the busiest artery in the world, the corridor through New Jersey. It was founded in 1766 and named Queen's College, originally, in honor of Charlotte, queen consort to George III. Beginning as an academy to train the clergy for the Dutch Reformed Church, it is now a major teaching and research university with all the disciplines.

Here urban America is under a microscope, with all its aspects exposed. Moreover, here we have a university set at the hub of six troubled urban centers—Camden, Trenton, Jersey City, Atlantic City, Newark, and Paterson—with all the symptoms of urban pathology found anywhere. Add to that the "fallout" from Brooklyn, Queens, Manhattan, and the Bronx. These are places to which Americans have rushed from Poland, Italy, Russia, Ireland, Hungary, Holland, Germany, and the rural South in waves since 1870. Then, following World War I the blacks came to escape Jim Crow and joblessness. After World War II and until now every flight from San Juan and Bogatá swells the numbers.

No clinic in America offers the laboratory situation that this mid-Atlantic corridor does, with respect to movement toward

160

the perfection of the American political experiment. If the possibility for such a community as I have presented exists at all, the signs should appear near where I have been for the past twenty years. And, even as slowly as such signs are emerging, I have faith that they will appear. My hope has been in education—not simply perfunctory schooling—but in real initiation into the uses of the mind. So, if one cannot be everywhere and do everything, start somewhere. At Rutgers I had the most fun for ten years teaching a course in "Studies in Afro-American Education," examining the chronological sequence of the education of blacks in America. This opened up the dialogue, and with very large classes we were able to explore, semester after semester, with teachers from throughout New Jersey and New York some of the stickiest and thorniest problems of the education of the black minority. Education is so crucial because this is the most definitive test of the capacity of America to function as a free, pluralistic, and democratic society. And I was in the center of it.

Here are some dimensions of this challenge. The Ford Foundation gave several schools a grant to develop courses in Afro-American studies. Such studies ran the gamut from one or two courses tucked reluctantly into a large history or English department, hoping no one would notice, to others that were fully blown departments with a dozen or so faculty members. Somewhere around 1978 the foundation called a meeting of all the recipients of the grants for accounting. We met in Aspen, Colorado, at the full expense of the foundation. Professor George Kelsey of Drew University and I were asked to be consultants, to listen for the best use of the funds, and to encourage its amplification. Well, on the first day of a weeklong session, the elected black chairperson asked the white Ford Foundation executive to leave the room while the blacks conferred and to return only when invited.

This was the watershed of many tributaries. For one thing, the blacks resented the appearance of a "plantation" arrangement, whether there was such or not; next, they felt vindictive toward the "power structure" that such a special effort had to be made to teach "black history"; and it was necessary for their own posture to show that they were not "Uncle Toms." I never felt such a chill in human relations as when I saw that white executive get up, red-faced as a beet, and slowly walk out. If at that level, among the best educated persons in the nation, such a fracture could occur, from where would hope come? My long involvement with the reconciling love of God in Jesus Christ caused me to feel wasted. (The chairperson who had asked the executive to leave had a doctor's degree in religion also.)

When I got to my room I asked myself, "How do we begin again? We are at ground zero." There is nothing to build on at all. Hate had hardened. Thank God we have since moved from that point, but let no one be mistaken. We must have many committed persons to labor in this quarry where the rock is hard indeed. I am here to stay. I will work for a community in America with whatever fragments are left around. To do otherwise violates everything I have settled for thus far!

At Rutgers we looked for any opening at all to alter the life chances of those locked into the ghettos of the six cities that I have mentioned. There they were—blacks and Hispanics with their own authentic cultures, lots of music, handclasps, black leather jackets, used Oldsmobiles, Cadillacs, Buicks, and Camaros, approved hair designs, code languages and good feelings. But they were not in colleges. They were working for minimum wages. They were shut out of jobs that tracked to good salaries. They were stealing for drugs. They were having babies like flies and going to jail "two on a mule." It looked like "fun town," but there were pain and hurt behind the mask of music and painted windows on GM "oldies." They were, untouched, on islands of despair in an ocean of opportunity and prosperity.

Clearly, their education needed to effect a greater change in their life chances. But they were hard to reach. It took a certain kind of streetwise, caring, fearless, communicative teacher to cope with them. And such teachers were few.

I recall that at the time another Ford grant was given to a

youth correction center in Pennsylvania to institute more relevant education for serious youth offenders. Again, I was asked
to form a team to assess what was happening. I recall getting
Dr. William Phillips, Edwin Bess, and Dr. Chester Jones, all in
the fields of education and social work, to make some visits
with me. As we passed one classroom door, a charming young
teacher looked kidnapped. Using the foulest language, the
young toughs had surrounded her, and one of them was pat-
ting her on her buttocks. They were out of control. We walked
in and settled them down, but she was thoroughly ill-suited for
such a task.

Across the hall a woman a full foot shorter, twenty pounds
lighter, and fifteen years older stood at her door as the same
gang walked by like tin soldiers. In her class they were building a colonial village, using tongue depressors for logs. Everyone went to work. It was as quiet as a morgue. She was ready
for that assignment.

We set out to recruit persons who had urban experience
equal to sixty or so semester hours of college. We put them
through a special sixty hours —with intern teaching—for a
master's degree in urban education, with various majors. They
need not have had any college at all—only experience that
would be sufficient background for our two-year program.
One student became a principal of an urban high school; another received a Ph.D. at Syracuse in government and is now
teaching at a Houston college; one has twice been named
teacher of the year in an urban high school; another became
a dean of students at Rutgers School of Engineering; one is a
counselor at Middlesex Community College, and all but one
out of forty are working closely with the very students whose
life chances need to be advanced.

Such programs were left over from the Johnson Administration and suffered from "new" initiatives with the Nixon
Administration. At the very time when we should be experi-
menting with all sorts of endeavors to penetrate the ghetto
walls and engage the minds of our desperate youth, we have
only more rhetoric about the death penalty and stiffer jail

terms. All the jails are full, and the problems in the streets are mounting. The middle class is moving farther out of town, and new thruways swish them around the problems to their sky-scrapers. We are spending $30,000 a head or better on recidivists, and the school districts that have the heaviest burden have the least support.

We need a better effort not only to cut back on crime, not simply to improve the quality of manpower and woman-power, not just to release the pressures on the jails, and not resignedly and begrudgingly to make cities safe and passable. More than all this, we want to see the lives of human beings attain their potential fulfillment. We want to see them honor and delight in their days, to have a future to look forward to, to enjoy the blessings of family life, to find deep satisfaction in a career that matches their talents and abilities, and to become a part of the "great conversation" about the quality of life on the planet and the attainable goals of humankind. This is the stuff of genuine community, converting these pockets of futility and despair into the flowering seedbeds of hope and enhancement of the life chances for all persons.

RECOGNIZING THE BARRIERS
TO COMMUNITY

Community demands that we remove the artificial barriers that permit xenophobia, estrangement, and a sense of other-ness. Apart from the separation that comes from extremes of poverty and cultural isolation, there is in America a yawning chasm between our minorities and the mainstream. There are individuals within minorities who have excellent relations with the majority community, by virtue of some special cir-cumstances, but we have a fog of prejudice that must lift somehow and give us a chance to work at the real issues that inhibit genuine community.

One Sunday morning at Abyssinian I welcomed some for-eign guests. Many were from France, as is usual at our church. Afterwards, a couple from Paris lingered and insisted on seeing me privately. My secretary, and "gatekeeper," obliged. The wife spoke, telling me how shocked she was at the warmth of our members, the ease she felt around a swarm of blacks, singing in church, and how much she enjoyed the dinner—our hypnotic smoked ham, with mouth-watering candied yams and corn on the cob; spoonbread with a golden hue and butter seeping from the center; collard greens cooked in Virginia cured ham hock that leave one speechless; and hot apple pie with a crust that melts on contact. She cried as she told me how people had lied to her about blacks in Harlem. In France they had warned her to stay out of Harlem. She had witnessed something that was completely off the screen of her mind. Then she poked her finger in my chest with emphasis and said, "As I sat and observed and listened, I cannot account for you at all!" That is to say, she knew Bill Cosby, Michael Jackson, Jesse Jackson, Oprah Winfrey, and Johnny Mathis, but she could not believe that there were enough literate blacks for Abyssinian to have one too! It is scandalous the ignorance that separates us!

It is not simply the racial estrangement that inhibits community, for we handle many of our minorities with ignorance. All "gays," for example, are not alike. They come in the same varieties as all of us. Being "gay" is not the principal aspect of their lives, except for the discrimination heaped upon them. There are offensive gay people as there are offensive heterosexual people. Genuine community requires us to see, beneath these statistical differences, persons with eligibility and talents. The total person must be recognized, not simply his or her hair, color, or sexual orientation.

I find myself, in my late sixties, still seizing every opportunity to participate in programs that give whites one more opportunity to understand who we are and the justification for our claims on absolute equality. My position in this regard is old-fashioned, but I see more than that in it. I know how easy it is for a white person to avoid *all* blacks and cling to the most specious and egregious prejudices. In 1980, Professor Carl Kaysen, the M.I.T. economist, invited me to join him and

165

several other Americans to conduct a seminar at Salzburg, Austria, at one of the classical old palaces converted into a conference center. I went looking for more opportunities to give persons of potential influence a chance to learn about blacks firsthand. Well, there were thirty-nine Europeans who knew only black celebrities, but many of the Americans present were equally strange to the black presence here. The questions asked in 1980 were shocking.

An ex-university president asked me sincerely why could not all American blacks do what my brothers and I had done, i.e., earn doctor's degrees in three different fields. I cannot accept such designations of uniqueness easily because I know of so many black families of equal and greater achievements, but I did respond to him that *not many whites* had done what we had. That was only to make a point. The interventions in our lives—parents educated in the 1900s by Pittsburgh United Presbyterians and a grandmother finishing Hampton in 1882—were rare; few persons of our age have had such undeserved benefactions. And, whether black or white, those who have had them should do better in life than those who did not. Race was *not* significant. The *nature of the interventions* was.

Goshen College in Goshen, Indiana, is off the beaten path, but a few years ago I spent one of the most rewarding visits of my life there. It was refreshing to be among whites who were voluntarily a minority—members of the Mennonite community—given to simplicity, sincerity, and service. In chapel they sang without an instrument. As the baton came down, they all landed on the first note with perfect harmony. They were thoroughly relaxed and secure in their manner. I learned so much about the importance of people being aware of who they were and why they were. And, again, I welcomed the hundreds of questions about my people and our future. All of this makes way for the sharing of values and the beginning of community.

Likewise, for several years I have gone to Calgary, Medicine Hat, Edmonton, and other smaller places in Alberta, Canada, for the Alberta Teachers Association. What am I doing in that cold weather in mid-February? Using one more available opportunity to "live" genuine community, living in their homes, playing with their children, and at night around a hot log fire getting dead serious about the human family and how we must share a sound basis for community.

In 1974, Professor Ernest Duncan of Rutgers, a popular mathematics textbook publisher and a native and proud New Zealander, arranged for me to spend three weeks touring those two marvelous islands with my eleven-year-old son. He personally bore my son's expenses. And why did we go? Once again, my opportunities to learn about New Zealand, its history and people, and to get to know Maori leaders, teachers and students were fantastic. The long conversations with the students were most revealing. They learned much about the struggles of our people for equality here, and I learned about the problems of their minority status in their own native land. Genuine community is an option, but it is not an inevitability. Persons committed to such a goal must work for it. I consider that every positive thing that I find to do for community and understanding has canceled at least one negative thought or deed against it. And with the providence of God the good thoughts and seeds may multiply.

It was for such a reason that I spent so much time participating in programs at the Jewish Theological Seminary with Jessica Feingold, Carlotta Damanda, and Rabbi Louis Finklestein. Jews and blacks have a long history of persecution, and, for whatever reasons, in New York City, there are suspicion and tension on the fringes of both communities. It is clear that if Jews feel that blacks will gain strides at their expense, they will become apprehensive. And when blacks see Jews in court fighting affirmative action, they automatically become their enemy. Much has to be done to create dialogue and understanding so that both groups can work to create a richer and more durable democracy. I have learned to see such real differences of opinion not as the *end* but as the *beginning* of more serious discussion.

167

When Zubin Mehta came to New York from Los Angeles to conduct the New York Philharmonic, he asked to talk with me. I had hired their music education director to be our minister of music, the late and beloved Dr. Leon Thompson. It appeared that Zubin Mehta had told Dr. Thompson of how the Los Angeles orchestra had gone into Watts, after the riots, and performed with local black choirs. I accepted the idea in a flash of having the New York Philharmonic, all 130 of them, come to Harlem and fill up Abyssinian twice for a concert—at 4 P.M. for dress rehearsal, attended by the schoolchildren and the senior citizens; and at 8 P.M. for the subscribers who paid only nominally to cover the stage construction each year. (No storage was available.) The orchestra came *gratis*, thankfully. Dr. Leon Thompson had performed a miracle.

Well, for six years running, Abyssinian was overflowed at 4 o'clock and 8 o'clock with the world's finest musicians playing the world's masterworks, topping it off by accompanying a reknowned gospel singer or playing old hymns on the violin or flute, with the orchestra providing a tapestry of violins and reeds in the background. Every year it was heavenly. A reporter asked me once why we did it. He implied that it looked silly to bring this expensive orchestra to Harlem's 138th Street and waste an evening. I asked him why he thought black folk filled the sanctuary twice each time! He shook his head. He had no understanding of the steps toward genuine community. The Jews in the orchestra had delighted in coming to a black Baptist church in Harlem to play Christian music and to eat "soul" food. This was one more opportunity for us to live community.

JUSTICE AND FAIRNESS: PREREQUISITES FOR GENUINE COMMUNITY

Those who commit themselves to the achievement of genuine community at home and in the world realize that justice and fairness are as much prerequisites to community as relief of suffering and removal of class and ethnic prejudices. Fairness and justice, in summary, require those like you and me, who inherited a favorable benefit system, to help those who inherited an unfavorable one to the point that they may be just as eligible and as capable as we are to achieve equal outcomes. Anything less is arbitrary and imposed by something less than fairness and justice.

Obviously, there are so many intangibles involved that one would hardly expect to see such a theory fully applied, but it points in the right direction. If we are not moving toward that kind of fairness, we are asking persons in the world to join us in community without any justification at all as to why they should accept both the position of poverty that they inherited and the position of affluence and well-being that we have.

Similarly, at home in America we are denied a sense of national community if Hispanics from smelly barrios, Native Americans from barren Midwestern villages, and blacks from a 247-year slave existence—and all of them living with many footnotes today—cannot understand why they had such a slow start at the scratch line. Thus, we are in the business now of evening up life chances to create as nearly as we can a *fair* situation, an even playing field, a straight scratch line. Community begins with fairness.

Things have changed a lot. Protests, court decisions, and Johnson era legislation have all helped. But sometimes only the climate changed. I was on my way to Central Michigan State University to accept an honorary degree when I noticed that on my flight sat Marian Anderson, the legendary contralto diva, the one whom Toscanini called the voice of the century. She was heading to Michigan State, also, and for the same reason. I felt like going back home, outclassed hopelessly! But nothing could stop me from easing over and begging for a brief audience. I hurriedly expressed my lifelong adulation of her, and we moved quickly to capture the few minutes of flight. I wanted her to go back to 1939 when the Daughters of the American Revolution refused to allow her to sing a concert in their Constitution Hall. What a travesty,

Constitution Hall! She was denied on account of her color; and, their membership was based on something as remote and incidental as their descent from a soldier in the Revolutionary War. What a basis for their community, and what a basis for excluding Marian Anderson! However, the climate of the nation had elevated beyond such, and Secretary of the Interior Ickes arranged for her to sing on Easter Sunday morning before 75,000 on the steps of the Lincoln Memorial. Mrs. Franklin D. Roosevelt canceled her D.A.R. membership, and other performers canceled their appearances there. The policy changed, and Marian Anderson sang there many times after that. The climate had changed.

Today the remaining residuals of injustice are not quite so poignant, but they are there. There is inertia in upscaling minorities in industry, government, the media, the fine arts, and education. So the black/white income gap is widening. And everyone is asking where the leaders are. They are all over; there are not just a few stellar ones. The problems are all over. Each state, each city has leaders. Adam C. Powell, Jr., was one black congressman; New York has four now, and every industrial, urban state has at least one. Mississippi even has one. Texas has one. New leaders are dispersed, as the problem is pervasive and endemic, not in one *locus*. Such a situation points to new strategies. Suffice it to say, as we press toward a real community, a national soul, a spirit of America, the injustices will remain a glaring impediment.

Perhaps the most serious threat to community will come from pressures abroad. We will not get out of this century without settling some old, old accounts. Already we have seen colonial French Indochina broken up, and the dust has not settled yet in Laos, Thailand, Cambodia, and Vietnam. South Africa is bound to erupt if the United States continues to be its silent partner in apartheid, lending money, selling military equipment, and buying exports. We are the world leader in this matter, and our position is not acceptable at all. In the Caribbean we have lost respect. We stuck with the leadership in Haiti, Cuba, and Nicaragua until it became a disgrace. We ended up the guardian of the deposed leaders of Iran, Haiti, and the Philippines when all other countries closed their airports to them. How do we accomplish this? We have gone around the world and gained the reputation of being a friend to the oppressors, and yet we continue the rhetoric of freedom, democracy, and compassion. Our fear of communism has driven us to positions that foster the thing we fear most. There *is* something between a nation of street beggars and diseased children, and a Marxist dictatorship; but such practical reforms and corrections seem elusive, and we are all hung up on ideologies.

On two occasions I found myself the object of stinging attacks on my country. I went to address the Caribbean Council of Churches in the early 1980s, and while my address was very well received, in the later discussions it was clear to me that the people of the islands where we all chase the sun want our tourist dollars but distrust our view of the world. In Sweden, at a recent conference on militarism and Third World needs, I heard a four-day chant on American moral failure in dealing with world poverty. We were placed on the side of the enemies. We came off no better than Russia. Alan Boesak, the South African leader, shared hours of discussion with me, and I learned that in South Africa we were seen as a friend of apartheid.

It is a strange feeling to be an American and to know something of the compassion that our people do have for the poor and then to attend a conference at Curacao or Upsala and have to spend my time alone in my room. I was dark-skinned, like so many of the conferees, but I represented a country whose government was always voting contrary to the interests and concerns of the world's poor and oppressed. All of my explanations sounded rapid, inane, and irrelevant. I went to my room and prayed that God would give us fresh direction.

Of course, the larger issue is that we have simply idolized big money so much that we have been blinded to the realities of the world. And everyone else can see this but us. Deregulation allows one to raise 10 percent of a fund for a hostile

171

takeover of a corporation, and borrow with junk bonds, at high risk and paying high interest, the remaining 90 percent. Then one sells off the companies' assets to pare down the debt while nervous housewives, widows, pensioners, and young parents investing for college hold their breath. With a lot of luck things stay glued together, and another instant billionaire is created. Otherwise, there is chaos that no one talks about. Who thought of such deregulation for such wild speculation? Money!

One day we were having a serious discussion on poverty at the headquarters of the war on poverty movement. Sargent Shriver, the energetic and idealistic husband of a Kennedy heir, Eunice, always a faithful patron of benevolent projects, was presiding. Shriver was comfortable around the poor, although his lifestyle was anything but impecunious. He empathized with persons who suffered. He had an old-fashioned Roman Catholic calling to respond to human need. A very religious person, he reflected this in all his thoughts and conversation.

But Fanny Lou Hamer was a Ruleville, Mississippi, civil rights fighter and a monitor of the war on poverty in Mississippi. When she spoke, with her face clear of any makeup, bearing a countenance of an innocent and determined witness, her voice was smooth and mellow like a soft bell sounding, but with the staccato of truth ringing. I gazed intently at every bend of her lips, every elevation of her eyebrow. She had been in the trenches a long time—beaten, shot at, jailed, and still stomping for the poor.

First, she jumped on some middle-class black sorority women for sending pigs to Mississippi paired off in crates, one male pig for each female pig. She said patiently, "Darling, we don't need but one boar for every ten or twelve sows. We don't marry them off in Mississippi. I don't know what y'all do in New York!" Then, she turned to Sargent Shriver and said, "And, you, what do you know about poverty? You've never been poor!"

With that, Shriver slammed his hands flat on the table,

sprang to his feet, lost his cool, and ranted on. He explained that he was sick and tired of defending his role. He had organized the war on poverty, fought to get it through congress, and did for the poor what the poor could not have done for themselves. "I'll be damned if I'm going to apologize for that." Then he pointed to me and said, "Another thing—I'm not rich. My wife is, but Sam Proctor has more than I do." I nearly fainted. I was drowning in debt. What happened was that she simply echoed the suspicions that poor people have of the rich; and even when persons of means are in the role of advocacy for the poor, their credentials have to be verified over and over.

This is especially true as we deal with the poor around the world. We have the ideas in America on which world community can be built: the innate worth of persons, government by the consent of the governed, personal freedom, due process of law, and rights that the state neither confers nor can deny. However, if our posture, voicing these ideas, is one of callous indifference toward those movements and persons who seek to relieve longstanding oppression, we forfeit the right to lead toward community.

The consequence is that we have to spend half of our national budget funding an arsenal for the free world. Not long ago as a trustee of the former Council on Religion in International Affairs, Robert Meyers, executive director of the Council, assembled some priests, bishops, rabbis, pastors, and assorted religionists to be briefed on NATO. I questioned the need, but I went for curiosity. In Brussels I saw the underground installations, the mammoth electronic charts that tracked moving weaponry around the world. In England, again, I saw the headquarters of the NATO fleet and how a few Trident submarines, with a range of thousands of miles and nuclear warheads, could level every city in Eastern Europe.

That amount of money, that level of technology, that application of genius could bring health, education, housing, and well-being to our world. The communists would have no clients. We could have freedom, pluralism, and democracy, and

173

keep our faith in God, too, in a world moving toward community.

The principle of fairness calls us also to consider our obligation to pass the planet that we inherited on to our waiting posterity without the ozone layer destroyed, forests depleted, arable land poisoned with radon, rivers and lakes thickened with chemical sludge, and the sea cluttered with urban, plastic waste. Democracy is people-oriented, government by the consent of the governed, and this consent embraces our grandchildren. We must be somebody *to* somebody in genuine community, and since we are in community with the next generation, we must be somebody to them.

One of the habits of my mind is to wonder what things will be like when all of us have folded our tents and slowly stolen away. Well, that procession following us is here, right now. Our Katie and David, and Herbie, Jr., Christopher, and Monica are here. I worry. Tuition and fees for some of the best colleges are now at $20,000 and rising. Homes in Eastern metropolitan areas are sitting right at $300,000. That is a mortgage of $2,500 a month for thirty years, and blest! Besides all of that, the average income for Americans is still in the $20,000 to $30,000 range, while congressmen make $89,500 and are plugging for $130,000. The national debt is in the trillions and climbing. We are about to pass on to our grandchildren an economy of paper-doll money. It will take a briefcase of bills to buy a loaf of bread, and they will live like many in the Depression, with three brothers or sisters and their spouses per house. I have been there. Once there were twelve of us using one bathroom!

Common sense, honesty, and imagination must come to the service of justice and cause this generation to exercise far more stewardship for the future than we do. It looks like no one's business in particular, but for our children's sake it must become everyone's business.

Finally, having been in university and church work for forty-four years now, I have noticed some things. In higher education we have no real agenda. We take adequate notes on what goes on, but we do not set goals or objectives worth pursuing. Once schools existed to promulgate the gospel, later to industrialize the nation, later to teach democracy, then to overtake Russia's lead in space. What is it now? Campuses look more and more like winter resorts, and students never are called together to rally about anything but football. Chapel assemblies are sparsely attended, and everyone is gone for commencement except the band, the choir, and the dining room help. There are no convocations for anything, for there is nothing about which to convoke! I would propose that the leadership should be bold in calling our intellectuals to the task of preparing our students to live in and lead toward a national community.

In the end this community will test our will to follow the principle of justice and fairness. This is the epitome of the moral life and the most profound application of the ethics of Jesus and the prophets of the eighth century B.C. in Israel. This should engage our best minds. Such a purpose would cast a shaft of light on everything that we do on campuses and chasten every discipline with an existential bent toward relevance. Our young people will appreciate an alternative to alcohol and drugs and a sense of purpose for their lives and for humankind. On our campus last year 350 abortions were performed. That is not unique. We have let our youth believe that nothing matters but money and hedonism. The pursuit of genuine community is a great alternative.

I cannot believe some of the attitudes that we have floating around our campuses influencing our young. One of the well-published economists of our area brought his son to our bowling alley. He sat at the table next to me, bowling in the lane next to where Steven, Sam, and I bowled. Sam was the Central Jersey high scorer, and the economist's son was only beginning. His ball stayed in the gutter. The father sat next to me with his back turned to me. I kept looking for an opening to speak and, further, to offer Sam's help to his son. Nothing. After sitting there for an hour, facing southwest, he stood up, tapped my shoulder, and said to me, "I want to commend you and your sons for not using any profanity and for not smoking!" The Holy Spirit held my tongue. He is a university leading light, completely oblivious of the most elementary aspects of community.

I continue to observe also that one of the most serious violations of fairness on our campuses is to gather social data always on a racial basis, publish it as such, and ignore other possibly causative variables. For example, how many inmates are in the Trenton State Prison? Twenty-two hundred. How many of them are black? Seventy-eight percent. Well, if you stop there, it looks like blackness gets people into prison. But go on counting. How many were reared without fathers? Eighty percent! How many were never taken to Sunday school? Ninety percent. How many were never taken fishing or to a ball game by their fathers? Ninety-five percent. Well, that being the case, it looks like we gather data any way we want to in order to perpetuate the stereotypes that we support. When we acknowledge finally that schooling is *not* value-free, we are ready then to select the most salient values to become the underpinning of our education. This is not a sectarian appeal but an appeal to the values that underlie our Declaration of Independence and our Constitution. They are the foundation for community.

In June, 1989, I retired from the pastorate of the Abyssinian Baptist Church and high on my agenda was preparation for the Lyman Beecher Lectures at Yale in February, 1990, and the filling of a chair in homiletics at Vanderbilt, 1990–1991. This is a wonderful way to bring the formal assignments of my career to a climax. I will use all of my time left, God willing, to preach the gospel of Jesus Christ and to advocate the pursuit of real community in America and in the world. We need educators, we need politicians, we need philosophers, but we need also those advocates, those prophets, those Elijahs who will speak the truth to Ahab, and those Nathans who will remain free to say to David, "Thou art the man." It is going to be exciting and rewarding to continue this odyssey and to search for the emergence of those "things of good report."